Texans
Behind the
News

Texans Behind the News

TEXAS JOURNALISTS OF THE TWENTIETH CENTURY

by

Dede Weldon Casad

EAKIN PRESS 🛡 Austin, Texas

To young writers of Texas,
who love words and aspire to be
journalists at the highest level of that profession.

FIRST EDITION
Copyright © 2000
By Dede W. Casad
Published in the United States of America
By Eakin Press
A Division of Sunbelt Media, Inc.
P.O. Drawer 90159 ⚏ Austin, Texas 78709-0159
email: eakinpub@sig.net
🖥 website: www.eakinpress.com 🖥
ALL RIGHTS RESERVED.
1   2   3   4   5   6   7   8   9
1-57168-321-6

Library of Congress Cataloging-in-Publication Data

Casad, Dede W., 1928–
    Texans behind the news : Texas journalists of the twentieth century / by Dede Weldon
Casad.
        p.   cm.
    Includes bibliographical references.
    ISBN 1-57168-321-6
    1. Journalists--Texas Biography. 2. Journalism--Texas--History--20th century.
3. Journalism--United States--History--20th century. 4. Journalists--United States
Biography.
PN4897.T43 C37   2000
070'.92'2764--dc21   99-
23793

Contents

Preface

Texans have always been in the news. Rarely is there a thirty-minute newscast from any of the major networks that does not have a story based out of Texas. Rarely is there a storyteller on that network who is not a Texan. Texas journalists have written their stories or filed their reports with dignity and grace for the entire twentieth century. This book is a tribute to their lives, and an appreciation for their work.

As of late 1999 all of them are still living. Most of them are as familiar as our own faces in the mirror. Most of them have covered the same stories. Each of them has been personally acquainted with six or more presidents of the United States. Sarah McClendon has known eleven.

With the exception of Walter Cronkite, Jim Lehrer, and Molly Ivins, each was born in Texas. Cronkite, Lehrer, and Ivins nevertheless had their journalistic grounding in Texas, so Texas claims them. They also claim Texas.

Their several careers cover the media gamut—from rural newspapers to modern anchors on television. Their lives also cover the bulk of the century. Each has his or her own story to tell. Retelling them now, in these short versions, certainly not meant to be definitive biographies, may whet the appetite for further reading. Their stories may also inspire young people to follow in their footsteps.

As I have worked on these mini-biographies it has occurred

to me repeatedly how normal and similar are their backgrounds. None of them aspired to be in the public eye. No, most of them only wanted to get the news to the public as quickly as possible. Their national fame has surprised each of them. Cronkite calls it luck. Moyers calls it coincidence. Donaldson calls it hard work. Whatever the reason, it seems like magic that people who started from humble beginnings could rise to the forefront of American journalism.

But isn't that the American dream?

First and foremost, journalists are writers. Each of them started writing with a newspaper (with the one exception of Sam Donaldson, who lacked early print experience). From there, they have become nationally syndicated columnists, members of the White House Press Corps, or anchors on major television programs.

Their stories are similar and dissimilar, but they all have a touch of Texas in their hearts.

Acknowledgments

I wish to thank each one of the profile participants. Without exception they each, sometimes with the help of their assistants, edited, corrected, and added to their manuscript. This assured me of the accuracy and authenticity I sought, and gave me a comfort level of presenting them in a true light.

They are truly Texans of the highest order. I salute every one of them.

Sarah McClendon

B iography, by definition, is written backwards. Never is the story of one's life written before the fact. How could it? A life must be lived before a true story about an honest-to-goodness person can be recorded. Only fiction can create make-believe people and places.

So who would have predicted back in 1910, in a small community of East Texas, that the Queen of Questions was being born? Certainly not her parents. Certainly not her friends. Certainly not Sarah.

Sarah McClendon was born the youngest of nine children—five boys and four girls. At the turn of the century her parents were living ahead of their time. Sarah's mother was a forerunner of today's feminist, always believing that young girls should have an education equal to young boys. Her father was an early version of Ralph Nader—a person who fought for the rights of consumers against corporations which sought to acquire financial gain no matter who got hurt. He supported the underdog in either a personal scrap or a political fight. His day job was working as a "piano merchant," then later as postmaster at the Tyler Post Office. Both parents were very political.

Growing up in such a large family, Sarah knew early on she must work for a living. Her brothers and sisters before her each had a job fresh out of high school. Sarah was supposed

1

Sarah McClendon
—Photo courtesy of Christy Bowe

to follow suit. Instead, she pushed on to junior college. While attending Tyler Junior College, she took a job as a book-keeper at a bank. It was so boring, she said, that "I felt as if I was feeding myself into a machine every day." A future with the bank held no interest for her.

A drama teacher at the college suggested to Sarah that she study journalism. Sarah was ready for anything new. So at nineteen years of age she pocketed her small savings and traveled to Missouri to begin her studies at the Missouri School of Journalism.

> *"I like to call myself a citizen journalist. I try to bridge the gap between big government and little people, because I believe journalism is a public trust. People who are well-informed will always do the right thing. The advantage in being this old is I don't have to look any-thing up. I already know most of it firsthand."*
>
> — Sarah McClendon

Sarah never questioned again what her life's work might be. The journalism bug bit her and left its telling scar. She loved journalistic reporting, particularly asking ques-tions. It was only later that she learned that any good reporter also has to be a good listener.

Upon graduation Sarah was told that in order to have a successful career in journalism she must find work in Chicago. Timid and unchar-acteristically shy, she made her way to the Windy City with the hopes of finding a job.

Chicago was crowded, scary, and intimidating. Sarah took up residence in a small hotel to search for the courage to face this new world. Being all alone in the big city without friends or family, Sarah was over-whelmed. She was so terrified of the fast pace, the busy streets, and the vast amount of strangers that she rarely left her hotel room. In a matter of days she boarded a train back to Texas.

Recovering from her failure in Chicago, Sarah took a second breath. She gathered up what little courage was left in her to call the editor of the local newspapers. There were two in Tyler: the *Tyler Courier-Times* and the *Tyler Morning Telegraph*. Sarah asked for a job.

Young women were not hired often as reporters in those days. So, much to her surprise, as well as to others, she snagged a job as a reporter. For over two years she worked under Carl Estes, her editor and mentor.

Sarah's first assignment was to help promote the building of a hospital in Tyler. This challenged her skills in every aspect of journalism—research, interviewing, and analysis. Crusading for a cause suited her personality to a tee, but often she would write articles that some city officials did not like. At one point Estes had to fire her because an influential citizen protested her work. She was out of a job for less than twenty-four hours. Estes hired her back the next day.

One of the most memorable events in Sarah's early training was logged on March 17, 1937. Eighteen miles east of Tyler, the New London school exploded. It was a sound heard around the world.

Sarah and a photographer by the name of Gunn rushed to the scene. It was a horrible sight. Two hundred and ninety-six people, mostly children, were blown to bits by a gas explosion.

Although stunned by what she saw, Sarah kept her head. She scrambled to find a telephone and called the International News Service to file her first report. It was the last call out of New London before the wires went down. Sarah then climbed into a truck to help the wounded as they made their way to the hospital.

Tyler's new hospital was to open the next day, but it opened a day early to accommodate the victims of this national tragedy. Sarah's interviews with the victims of the tragedy during the next few weeks tested and refined her reporting skills.

When Estes left Tyler for an editorial position in another city, Sarah's job was in jeopardy, even though she had worked for the two Tyler papers for over eight years. When the new editor arrived, he let her go.

For a short time she became a regional correspondent for newspapers in Houston, Dallas, Fort Worth, and Shreveport. After a year she accepted an offer with the *Beaumont Enterprise* in Beaumont, Texas.

Her tenure as a reporter at the Beaumont paper was cut short due to the United States' involvement in World War II. It was 1941, and the war in Europe was brewing strongly. It was at this time that Sarah remembered a childhood promise she had made to herself.

In 1918, when she was seven years old, two of her brothers had left to go into the army in World War I. At that time she swore she would someday be a soldier.

So, in 1941, much to her family's disbelief and serious disapproval, Sarah went down to the recruiting office and volunteered for the newly formed WAAC. She sold her clothes to pay off her debts, thinking the army would supply what she needed.

Sarah had defied her parents and shocked her friends for the second time. The first time was when she converted to Catholicism while in college after being raised an Episcopalian. She said, "My parents and friends accepted the fact that I'd converted to Catholicism, and bore with me when I threatened to become a nun, but no 'lady' joined the army." Nevertheless, Sarah never looked back.

Once again, Sarah McClendon left Texas, this time heading for Des Moines, Iowa—not to military intelligence as she had applied, but to basic training as a lowly recruit.

Withstanding the rigors of army life and disliking the food, Sarah managed to complete basic training successfully.

She was so successful that soon after entering the WAAC, she received a recommendation to Officers' Candidate School.

Sarah's natural, gung-ho tendencies began to emerge and immediately served her well in the army. Declaring she did not know how she survived the studies at OCS because she couldn't even read a map correctly, she nevertheless graduated as a second lieutenant. When her superior asked if Lieutenant McClendon would be interested in a transfer to the WAAC Training Center at Fort Oglethorpe, Georgia, she screamed, "You bet!" The temperature was twenty-one degrees below freezing in Des Moines at the time.

Missing out on the top job of setting up the new WAAC office at Fort Oglethorpe, Sarah was assigned to unite and deploy women where they could best serve. At that time women were needed for desk jobs that relieved the male soldiers for active duty overseas.

Sarah could not have been happier. She put on her public relations hat and programmed special events. Among them was a debutante ball, complete with army officers parading around the hall in the "grand march." Another was a party celebrating the anniversary of the founding of the Women's Army Auxiliary Corps. The giant birthday cake was too big to go through the double door. Sarah has fond memories of those days.

A telegram soon came announcing the relocation of the WAAC headquarters to the Pentagon in Washington, D.C. Sarah McClendon was tapped specifically to be the liaison between the WAAC and the War Department Bureau of Public Relations. She later became the first WAAC to work under the U.S. Army Surgeon General's Office. Her job was to furnish pictures and stories to national publications and newspaper editors, making sure that what they printed was accurate and non-classified. While in Washington she obtained a visitor's membership to the Women's National

Press Club. Friends made at the club were to have an impact on Sarah's life in years to come.

While still in the army, Sarah met her future husband, John Thomas O'Brien, a paper salesman. They married after a short courtship, but the marriage proved to be a mistake. John left her for a former friend, but not before Sarah discovered she was pregnant. Two realities faced her: Her army career was over (in those days the WAAC did not allow women to have children while on active duty). And she would be forced to work to support her child.

Alone and without a job, Sarah took back her former name, gave birth to her beautiful baby, whom she named Sally, and in nine days she set out to find a job as a reporter. Her first interview was with Bascom Timmons, a noted correspondent who ran a large, well-established news bureau from an office in the National Press Building. He hired her and helped her to become the Washington correspondent for the *Philadelphia Daily News.* This was the start of the career that has now spanned the terms of eleven presidents.

Within the first month Sarah McClendon found herself, complete with a White House Press pass (a rarity for women in those early years), standing in the crowded office of President Franklin D. Roosevelt. He was holding a press conference.

In those days reporters were not equipped with electronic devices as they are today. They wrote their report while standing up, taking notes on another reporter's back or after they left the conference. Also, reporters deferred to authority with timidity and respect. At her first press conference Sarah listened while the more experienced reporters asked their questions politely. If a reporter had questioned the president's answers or challenged him in any way, as is done today, it would have been certain career suicide.

Raised a Democrat and an Episcopalian, Sarah now found herself a Catholic, and needing to remain as quiet as possible. Her families were staunch Democrats, but they disagreed with Roosevelt on many issues. Standing in front of him now, Sarah felt uncomfortable and conflicted. Nevertheless, she was awed by his powerful presence and spellbound by his enormous influence.

Roosevelt was so formidable that Sarah, as a news reporter, often felt uncomfortable and out of place in the White House and the Congress. But it was from the back row of the balcony that she began to learn about politics from the top of government.

By the time Harry S. Truman became president, Sarah had overcome her awkwardness. She attended press conferences with regularity and soon began to risk asking questions.

When the war was over and military men were returning home to their jobs, Sarah once again found herself cast out. Her boss, Timmons, had to give the returning servicemen their old jobs and suggested that "you should have your own news bureau." He even went further out on a limb and offered her some of his clients to get her started.

From that day until this, Sarah has operated her own business as a Washington correspondent for newspapers around the country. In the process of building the McClendon News Service she built her reputation. It's a reputation spiked with candor and colored with a no-nonsense directness. Some say she made a career out of "hijacking presidential press conferences with picayune policy questions, venting her ire about whatever injustice or inequity preoccupied her."

Sarah explained, "Why, then, did I get a reputation for baiting a President whom I generally and genuinely— admired? . . . I felt it was high time to push my career to a new level of prominence. I had noticed that other female reporters gained attention by developing a distinctive sense of style: May Craig with her trademark hats, Esther van Wagoner Tufty with the aristocratic ways that had Washington calling her 'the Duchess.' It was time for me to not just attend the conferences and ask an occasional question, but to make my presence known in an ongoing way. I did not intend to be confrontational. But it did not work exactly the way I had planned."

On a personal level, as only one of a half dozen female correspondents in Washington at the time, she had to work harder to be accepted into the all-male profession. It took her twenty-seven years to break the male-dominated barrier and be accepted as a member of the National Press Club. She had submitted her application in 1955.

No other reporter has had more personal attacks upon her work than Sarah. Every president, from FDR to Bill Clinton, has had to deal with her biting tenacity in getting a proper answer.

Her relationship with President Truman was congenial enough. She found him likable, but shocking at times. He was a man of few words—direct, plain, realistic. He impressed the Press Corps by immediately moving the press conferences from the Oval Office, where FDR held them, into the Indian Treaty Room. The room was larger, so that everyone could sit down and be in a better position for taking notes. President Eisenhower followed with the regular press conferences.

During the Eisenhower administration, Sarah perfected her skills as the Queen of Questions. She embarrassed the president so many times, with seemingly regional questions, that Eisenhower's aides suggested he quit calling upon her. Eisenhower also never fully understood what her news service entailed—that it represented many papers across the country. One day when Sarah waved to get attention and was finally called upon, she did as all reporters do, gave her name and the paper she represented. So confused by her ever changing newspaper title, the president stopped her one day in mid-question and asked, "Do you get fired every week and go to work for a different paper?"

Her questions made her so unpopular with her colleagues and the administration that she was accused by them of causing Eisenhower's heart attacks, or at least his high blood pressure.

Sarah considered herself a friend of John F. Kennedy until her questions annoyed him so much that he wound up accusing her of everything short of treason. The straw that almost broke the president's back was when Sarah landed her now famous bombshell on him.

That day the press conference was held in the State Department auditorium because he was such a popular president, and press conferences were well attended. When finally recognized, Sarah stood up and asked why two long-time State Department officials, who were at that moment being seriously investigated by Congress as security risks, had been assigned to the task force to reorganize the State Department's Office of Security.

The president was stunned. He hemmed and hawed but finally said he thought both gentlemen had been thoroughly cleared, then ended up scolding Sarah for her question.

The question caused a national outcry. *The New York Herald Tribune* branded her as a "gadfly," and *Time* magazine called her a "president baiter." The reactions were so severe that Sarah lost friends, clients, and valuable contacts.

But she survived because she was right.

Sarah was no less determined in her relationship with President Lyndon Johnson. Johnson had previously said to her, "Sarah, your name is now a household word," and was immediately on his guard when he opened up his own press conferences. It was a case of two Texas longhorns duking it out. Sarah admits she was "one of those who irked Lyndon, who never soft-soaped him or smoothed over his wrinkles in my stories. I was never part of that group. I was a friend, not a lapdog."

For her troubles Johnson saw to it that some Texas newspapers dropped her. Those that had been with her for years terminated her services without notice or explanation. She was deeply hurt, but her business, once again, survived.

President Richard Nixon treated her questions differently. For instance, when she asked the president about "a particular bureaucrat, named Shillito, who was wasting the taxpayers' money and promoting his friends," the president answered, "I don't know the gentleman, but after that question, I am going to find out who he is." The headlines the next morning stated, "Mr. President . . . Then Came Sarah With the Shillito Stiletto." Once again, Sarah had managed to clip the wings of an unsuspecting president.

In spite of this, Nixon invited her for an extended one-on-one interview with him as they traveled together on a three-hour flight to Texas. This was a real coup for any reporter in those days.

President Gerald Ford was the "nice guy" to the press, and Sarah allowed him space. Then came President Ronald Reagan. Reagan was the only president to invite her to a White House luncheon. He knew how to charm the reporters. When Sarah had to take a four-month leave, due to a hip operation, Reagan not only called and asked how she was doing while she was in the hospital, but on her return mentioned that there had been no press conferences because he was waiting for Sarah to come back.

But even he did not escape the searing questions that Sarah felt obligated to ask. Neither did President George Bush. Bush often lectured the press on their attitude toward him and once he had to tell Sarah, "Sarah, I won't take your question until you sit down and ask it in a dignified manner." She, however, managed the last word: "You won't answer my question if I ask in a dignified manner, Mr. President."

Such was the traditional exchange of barbs and bites between the Queen of Questions and the men who happened to be president of the United States.

In two books she recounts her experiences on the beat of the White House. Her first book, published in 1978, is entitled *My Eight Presidents,* and the other, published in 1996, is *Mr. President, Mr. President!*

Now approaching the age of ninety, Sarah is still on the beat. Since her hip surgery she has had to walk with a walker and often reverts to a wheelchair. She was one of the first to greet President Bill Clinton after his election, and remained enthusiastic about his presidency.

No other person has had the personal exchange, the direct contact, the ability to vex and madden as many presidents as has Sarah McClendon. "Those questions" that established prickly face-offs with presidents, congressmen, Cabinet members, and other public officials have had their impact. Sarah herself says, even at this age, "I've got to keep going. I don't see many reporters watching government the way I do."

Sarah McClendon is a legend in her own time. As a champion for women in journalism as well as business, as a devotee of the army services, as a courageous single mother, Sarah has made her mark. She is truly one remarkable woman—and an incorrigible Texan!

Walter Cronkite

Walter Cronkite was not born in Texas. Too bad, for he is a Texan, heart and soul, and for this reason he should not be omitted from the list of major Texas journalists. Actually, the "granddaddy" of all national television journalists was born in St. Joseph, Missouri, on November 4, 1916, to a young dentist and his wife.

The Cronkite side of the family came from Dutch stock, while Walter's mother's family came from Bavaria. Through intermarriages with English and Scottish immigrants, the Cronkites' lineage evolved into a classic American mix by the turn of the century.

Walter has fond memories of his childhood. Walter's grandfather owned a pharmacy, or in those days, a drugstore. It was around his grandfather's drugstore that he learned lessons for a lifetime. It was during the summer months while playing around the store that the newspaper business began to intrigue him. At the age of six he noticed boys hawking the *Kansas City Times* on various corners of his neighborhood. He distinctly remembers the Extra Edition the boys hawked announcing the death of President Warren G. Harding. Walter dreamed of the time when he would be old enough to hawk newspapers.

When Walter was scarcely seven years old, he secured his first job—going door to door with a sack over his shoulder

13

Walter Cronkite
—Photo courtesy of Steve Friedman

selling the *Liberty* magazine. The magazine sold for five cents. Every magazine sold meant a penny in his pocket.

His second job was back to his first interest, newspapers. He sold the *Kansas City Star* Sunday paper. On Saturday night he would ride the streetcar downtown to the newspaper office. He would purchase ten papers, since that was all he could carry, then catch the streetcar back to his neighborhood corner where he would sell his papers. Every Saturday night after car fare he netted ten cents.

When Walter was ten years old, his family moved to Houston, Texas. His father went into partnership with another dentist. But every summer Walter would return to Kansas City to visit his grandparents.

> *"The deadline was a tough one for the 'CBS Evening News' staff . . . I insisted that our newsroom be our studio because only then could I enforce my philosophy—namely, that we were a medium that should pride itself on our technical ability to get on the air instantly, whenever news broke. Our mantra was that we had a deadline every minute."*
>
> — Walter Cronkite

An especially traumatic event which happened when Walter was a young boy stamped a lifelong fear of fire into his psyche. It took place at the Electric Park, an amusement park in Kansas City. The park was located only a few blocks from his home. One night the park caught fire. As he stood on his porch, his eyes stared at the turning ferris wheel. Flames were lashing up and around its sides. Some grease then caught fire on the two parallel tracks of the Greyhound Racer roller coaster. Red and yellow flames raced up and down, sparking a spectacular display of fireworks. About that time the fun house collapsed in a horrifying bonfire. To young Walter the sight was overwhelming, the heat suffocating, the sounds deadening. He stood transfixed, etching the scene in his memory.

That picture never left him. To this day Walter can still

see the terrifying sight in his mind's eye. The event made such a lasting impression upon him that even today he is careful when entering a building to check out the location of the fire escapes.

Walter also received several lessons in human relationships from his dad. One evening Walter's father and his dental partner, whom we shall call Dr. Smith, were visiting on the porch of Dr. Smith's home in the uppercrust neighborhood of River Oaks. Dr. Smith had ordered some ice cream from the drug store, and the black delivery boy was approaching with the order in hand. Suddenly, Dr. Smith stopped his conversation. When the boy reached the first step, Dr. Smith charged out of his chair. Without warning he proceeded to hit the youth square in the face. "That'll teach you, nigger, to put your foot on a white man's front porch."

Walter's father was so startled and incensed that he immediately called for his wife and son and said, "Helen, Walter, we're going now." Ignoring an offer from Dr. Smith for a ride, the family stalked away into the night and made the long trek home on foot. Walter's father subsequently broke his partnership with Dr. Smith, and the lesson was not lost on young Walter. He often remembered that first lesson in injustice during the sixties and seventies, when America was in the throes of racial confrontations.

As a typical teenager Walter occupied himself in other activities besides his constant desire to have money in his pocket. He was a Boy Scout and a member of the DeMolay. He enjoyed roller hockey, bicycle polo, tennis, and golf. Since Houston was close to the Gulf of Mexico, he relished swimming and occasional aquaplaning.

On reading a story in *American Boy* magazine, while he was in junior high school, Walter decided he wanted to become a foreign correspondent. He edited his high school paper and worked summers as a copyboy on *The Houston Post*. At the University of Texas he helped pay for his expenses by working at the state capitol bureau of the Scripps-Howard Papers. He also did a daily sportscast for a local radio station. After two years at the university, he dropped out of school to take a full-time job on *The Houston Post*. He later regretted not completing his formal education, but Cronkite was eager to get on with his career.

From *The Houston Post*, Cronkite joined the United Press.

In less than two years, the UP had transferred him from Houston, to Kansas City, to Dallas, to Austin, and finally to El Paso. This experience grounded him as a Texas journalist.

While covering the Dallas beat one of the worst trage-dies in Texas history occurred. The New London school ex-ploded. Receiving the news, Walter and the Dallas bureau manager took off for East Texas. For forty-eight hours Walter covered the horrifying scene, a devastating picture of total destruction. He watched as one by one, 294 shattered bodies, most of them children, were dug out of the rubble. Adding to the nightmare was the inability to gain accurate information. Only chaos prevailed. It was days before the true facts behind the disaster could be published.

At that time the reporter's job was hampered in many ways. For example, there were no car radios nor car tele-phones. A reporter had to scramble to get a telephone line out to file his report. This experience, as ghastly as it was, condi-tioned Walter for the future. It was only the first of many cata-strophic events he was to witness and report upon firsthand.

His El Paso assignment with the UP was short lived. WKY, out of Oklahoma City, wanted him to return to radio sports broadcasting. The job was not the appeal. A girl was. Being in Oklahoma brought him closer to his one and only girlfriend, Betsy Maxell, who lived in Kansas City.

In Oklahoma, Walter's assignment was to broadcast all of the Oklahoma University football games. When the foot-ball season was over, he advanced to the newsroom to de-liver the nightly news.

The lure of the love of his life sent him back to Kansas City. After a long courtship, Walter finally convinced Betsy to marry him. So on March 30, 1940, the two were married at the Grace and Holy Trinity Episcopal Church in Kansas City.

World War II then caught Walter's attention and imagination. Remembering his desire to be a foreign correspondent, he rejoined the United Press International with a request to go to Europe.

His first assignment was as part of a convoy of twelve military ships transporting the first wave of United States Army Air Force pilots to England in preparation for the war with Germany. There was much confusion as to Cronkite's role. The army had assigned him the emblem "C" to be worn on his left arm. Most army personnel thought he was a chaplain. It was some time before the men made the transition in their minds that "C" meant correspondent.

It took longer for the military to realize the importance of the role of a foreign correspondent. Keeping the folks at home informed as to the progress of the war was not a high priority for the military. Not only that, most military personnel rarely knew how difficult it was even to get a story filed through security in those first days.

Walter's next assignment was to cover the invasion of North Africa. On this trip he was riding with the navy on the battleship *Texas*. His experience with General Patton is recorded in Cronkite's biography, *A Reporter's Life*.

For the bulk of the war, Cronkite was based in London. He traveled from time to time with the various forces to the front lines for a closer view of the war. Often, he hopped on an airplane that was assigned to strafe a particular enemy target. Once, he was even assigned as a backup gunnery man. When he found German planes buzzing around, he manned his gun and cut loose. He wasn't sure he hit the planes directly, but at least he kept them at bay. When his plane landed back in London, he had to climb his way out of the waist-high pile of expended .50-caliber shells he had fired.

On D-Day Cronkite was ordered to stay in London to write the lead story. But in the hours before the allied landing he grabbed an opportunity to fly with the bombers over the Normandy beaches. In the subsequent years of the war in Europe, he covered the Normandy campaign, landed with the 101st Airborne Division in the Netherlands, covered the Battle of the Bulge, and reported on the German surrender in northwest Europe. His many firsthand, eyewitness reports— born out of his personal willingness to view dangerous events close up—won him high praise in his profession and established him as a crackerjack journalist.

Immediately after the war, Cronkite covered the war crimes trials in Nuremberg. Then he was sent to Moscow to be a foreign correspondent. At the time only seven news-paper and radio correspondents made up the "colony" of reporters.

Living conditions were all but primitive. In those postwar days most families lived in an apartment with three or four other families. Since Walter had Betsy with him, the Cronkites managed a small apartment with four rooms. Food was hard to come by, as well. Each day Betsy would search for food. If there was a gathering of the American correspondents for any social event, it was always at the Cronkites' because their apartment butted up against the boiler room. It was the only warm place in the building.

As a correspondent with the responsibility to report the facts about the Russian diplomatic policies and activities, Cronkite found it hard to gain the truth. There was so much suspicion surrounding Americans and their intentions that no one would trust them with the truth. Russians even distrusted each other. One informant would quickly discredit another Russian in order to establish his own worthiness. Cronkite searched out information from the highest authorities to the taxi drivers, but inevitably the stories were inconsistent, if not blatantly untrue.

On a trip to Gorky, Cronkite met one of his most "unforgettable characters." He was an elderly gentleman with whom the correspondent played chess on board the ship. Cronkite remembers that the man was pleasant and gregarious. He wore a tieless, buttoned-up shirt and the leather-billed khaki hat of an old revolutionary. He and Cronkite played and discussed issues as best they could under the limitations of the language barrier. As they parted on the last day of the journey, Cronkite finally asked the man what he did. He answered, "I'm one of the people who run this country. I'm a member of the KGB."

The Cronkites stayed in Moscow reporting for the United Press for two years. When Betsy became pregnant with their first child, she returned to Kansas City. Walter remained for four months to fulfill his obligations before returning to the States.

The excitement of radio newscasting still appealed to Walter. When the offer came to go to Washington to open a bureau for KMBC and a consortium of other Midwestern radio stations, he was ready to go. But it wasn't long before the Korean War arose, and Edward R. Murrow hired him away to work for CBS.

Thus began a long career with CBS. His first job was in radio, reporting for the six o'clock news. Then Cronkite was asked to sit at the news desk in front of a television camera.

Television was in its infancy at the time. No TelePrompters were available. So instead of writing out his copy, Cronkite ad-libbed it. His script was simply a list of subjects on which he was to report. Fortunately, he was adept at remembering names and precise figures. He was also a natural conversationalist, and his talent for finding the essence of a story established the style that would long be his trademark.

Cronkite's philosophy in reporting news is, "I am the

front page, the columnist and analysis are the back page." What he meant by this was that he would never take a biased viewpoint in his reporting. "Facts, facts, facts" was his motto.

Only twice did he veer from this philosophy. Once was during the Vietnam War. The other time was when he fortuitously established a way in which Egypt's President Anwar Sadat and Israeli's Prime Minister Menachem Begin could and would meet. Both of these events happened long after Walter Cronkite was well established as the voice of CBS, and his name had become a household word.

Early in his network career he was sent to cover the coronation of Queen Elizabeth II. This was perhaps one of the most challenging assignments he had undertaken because of the competition that was mounting between the networks, compounded by the difficulty of getting filmed coverage across the ocean. Each network vied to be the first to reach the public with the news. In those days there was no way electronically to send pictures to the waiting public. Film had to be shipped across the Atlantic by airplane. Cronkite and his crew devised a plan to have the newsreels edited and numbered, then shipped to the waiting network through a Canadian airline that was scheduled to arrive in New York prior to the American airlines. As luck would have it, the Canadian plane had to stop in Canada before going on to New York. Also, when they arrived in New York, the well-marked newsreels of the entire ceremony had been scrambled. Picking one at random, the newscasters shoved it on the air. Fortunately, it was the one of the coronation ceremony itself. The other networks had only the tapes of the early events of the day and did not get to show the actual coronation until the tape with those shots arrived. Thus, CBS viewers saw the coronation first.

Walter Cronkite was the first "anchorman" to hold that title. So pervasive was the title that during the early days of broadcast news the anchormen in Sweden were called "cronkiters."

About this same time the networks were adopting the practice (that still holds today) in which dual anchors host the news at the Democratic and Republican National Conventions. Walter Cronkite was the key man for CBS for every convention with one exception. Due to the popularity of Huntley-Brinkley on NBC, Cronkite's ratings were in a slump, and he was not allowed to head the team for the 1964 convention.

On September 2, 1963, Cronkite had an exclusive interview with President Kennedy in which the president stated that the success of the war in Southeast Asia would ultimately be determined by the Vietnamese themselves and their own willingness to fight to the end. A short two-and-a-half months later Cronkite reported that Kennedy had been shot in Dallas. As he had to announce the young president's death, Cronkite stripped off his glasses as he choked back a tear. Some thought he was not as professional as he should have been. History has proven them wrong. Cronkite's human characteristics have endeared him to the public.

After the death of Kennedy the public shifted its interest to Vietnam. Several times Cronkite made personal trips to the front. On his last return he predicted a stalemate between the North and South Vietnamese. He reported, "We have been too often disappointed by the optimism of the American leaders, both in Vietnam and in Washington, to have faith any longer in the silver linings they find in the darkest clouds." This was a pivotal statement in convincing President Johnson not to seek reelection. He said, "If I've lost Cronkite, I've lost middle America." Subsequently, Johnson announced his retirement from the presidency and politics. For the first time Walter Cronkite diverted from his role as newscaster. He had become a pundit as well.

Cronkite was to know and interview every president from Truman to Clinton. He especially liked the president from Texas, Lyndon Johnson. Early on, while Johnson was senate majority leader, Cronkite frequently saw him at the Capitol along with another Texan, House Speaker Sam Rayburn.

Johnson was not comfortable speaking to the press. He was often hostile and reticent. Due to Cronkite's easy manner, his television interviews with the president became more conciliatory. Cronkite viewed Johnson as larger than life, and Johnson, to his credit, realized the power and influence Cronkite had on the minds and hearts of the American people.

"Uncle Walt," "Old Faithful," "The Iron Man," and a number of other endearing terms have been used to describe Walter Cronkite, and each is justified. His grandfatherly appearance made him, as *Time* magazine said, "The single most convincing and authoritative figure in television news." Another observer stated that he was as "comfortable as old slippers." For almost twenty years the American public watched him in the evening, trusting his news, and nodding in agreement with his now famous sign off—"And that's the way it is."

Cronkite conducted scores of high profile interviews and covered many historic news stories, such as the Watergate scandal and the meeting of Sadat and Begin in Israel. He accompanied President Eisenhower back to the beach at Normandy and President Nixon on his summit visits to Beijing and Moscow. He was the chief correspondent for many CBS programs, such as "Reports about South Africa," "Eisenhower," and "D-Day Plus 20 Years." He hosted the "Eyewitness to History," "Twentieth Century," and "Twenty-First Century" series as well as the "You Are There" documentaries.

One of his most rewarding moments in television was when he covered the space shots. Never too astute in physics or science, Cronkite often wonders what his professor at the University of Texas, who had failed him in first-year physics, would have thought of his announcing the highly technical procedures of the space explorations—especially the moon walk! Cronkite will tell you that he worked hard to understand the mechanics of space flight. For instance, "One of the oddities he learned in order to explain spacecraft maneuvers was that the spacecraft, in relation to the earth, slowed down by speeding up. By accelerating, the craft moved higher, away from the earth, and thus took longer to orbit the earth—in effect, slowing down. By slowing down it fell closer to earth, thus speeding around it faster."

The most memorable, as well as historic, moment for Cronkite was when Neil Armstrong, announcing that the *Eagle* had landed, stepped onto the moon's surface. Cronkite admits he was speechless for the first time. All he could mutter was, "Oh, boy! Whew! Boy!" Words, he said, which were surely not very profound, but would, nevertheless, be recorded for the ages. In an interview with Charles Osgood in 1997 on the CBS program *Sunday Morning,* Cronkite admitted that not getting to go on a space mission was the biggest disappointment in his life. Even at eighty he said that if he was physically able to go, he would jump at the chance.

This love of adventure is easy to understand when we know about his other dare-devil experiences. Walter and Betsy took flying lessons before they were married. Walter also loved cars even as a young boy. When he was older and finally making enough money to buy a racing car, he entered speed racing contests. Acutely aware of the danger, he believed, for a time, that the thrill of driving 150 miles per hour outweighed the risk. But after several years and some near misses on the track, he gave it up in consideration of his wife and children. Sailing then challenged his restless spirit. The ocean became his new adventure. He volunteered in 1982 to ride the Woods Hole Oceanographic Institute's three-man *Alvin* 8,500 feet down to the thermal rifts southeast of Mexico's Cabo San Lucas. Cronkite writes, "This was the second trip following the discovery of these volcanic vents and the scientifically shattering fact that there were animals down there—great worms, spiny crabs, and huge clams—that lived by chemosynthesis, their energy supplied by chemicals rather than a food chain sustained by the sun."

Throughout his career Walter Cronkite has never shirked from adventure. Be it in the midst of a war zone, the jungles of the Amazon, or flying to the ice caps, Cronkite relishes the experience. One can now understand his disappointment in not being asked to join the astronauts in outer space.

Cronkite is proud of the documentaries he produced while at CBS. One of the most noted was the pioneer environmental series "Can the World Be Saved?" Another was "Walter Cronkite's Universe." And one that every American remembers, "You Are There," a program that reconstructed historical events as if CBS actually had covered them at the time those events happened.

Since his retirement in 1981, after almost twenty years as the chief anchor and managing editor of CBS, Cronkite has been shackled by what he calls his "golden handcuff." His severance from CBS stipulated that he could not work for another major network during his lifetime. This forced him to move his work to cable and public television. Every year on PBS he hosts the New Year's concert of the Vienna Philharmonic. And for the past several years he has hosted the President's Award Evening at Washington's Kennedy Center. He has recently created his own documentary film company that supplies programs to the Discovery Channel, including "The Great Books," "Understanding Science," and the news-oriented "The Cronkite Report."

Walter Cronkite has always held definite views about journalism, especially television journalism. He believes in a responsible press, but feels that media responsibility does not depend upon individual journalists as much as it does on the owners of the network. He also believes that television journalism should not take the place of a good newspaper. People should gain more in-depth knowledge by reading news analyses, he says. The trouble with the modern news-cast is the "sound bite," usually a partial sentence of five to ten seconds. He believes that this truncated form of information is detrimental to the political process. No adequate message can be given in such a short amount of time. This, Cronkite insists, is a weakness in today's television news industry.

Maintaining his philosophy of accuracy and truth above all else has made people, even after his departure from the evening news, say, "I just won't believe it until Walter Cronkite says so."

Now in his eighty-third year, Walter Cronkite can look back on a full life with satisfaction. For over fifty years he has covered every major American news event, political campaign, space shot, assassination, political convention, election, war, summit, and peace talk. He was the first newsman to receive the Gold Medal of the International Radio and Television Society. And in 1981 President Jimmy Carter honored him with the Medal of Freedom. No other man who has spanned this century can catalog such a career. He is the author of *Challenge of Change,* a series of three coffeetable books (with Ray Ellis) based on his boating experiences, and his autobiography, *A Reporter's Life.*

Cronkite and his wife have three children—Nancy, Kathy, and Chip—and four grandchildren. Kathy and two of the grandchildren live in Austin, Texas.

We probably have not heard the last of Walter Cronkite. With his Texas "can-do" training and predilection to innovation, he will be on television, giving us historical perspective on whatever is of current interest and reminding us . . .

AND THAT'S THE WAY IT IS!

Liz Carpenter

At seventy-nine years of age, Liz Carpenter maintains that life gets better all the time. When she was born in Salado, Texas, in 1920 only about two hundred people inhabited the community. Yet even then life was good. Salado was a stopover on the original cattle trail northward from San Antonio. It still maintains the flavor of the old days. The famous Stagecoach Inn that has housed travelers since pioneer times is still open and a favorite place to eat and visit.

When Liz was a child, the world beyond Salado beckoned. From the upstairs gallery of her grandparents' house, Liz would sit and watch the enticing world. She listened to the cars passing by along an interstate highway in the distance and wondered what her future held.

Liz's maternal grandfather, E. Sterling C. Robertson, was a founding father of the community. He loved the rolling hills and decided to settle. In 1853, he built his home—now known as the Robertson house. It is the oldest home in Texas to be occupied by the same family.

Primarily interested in education, Robertson started Salado College, an institution that offered a classical education. Later, as a member of the Constitutional Convention of 1875, Robertson helped write the article providing free public education for children.

Liz Carpenter
—Photo courtesy of Jim Dougherty

Also in 1875, Liz's great aunt Luella, then only eighteen years old, risked speaking in public. She stood on Salado Hill and spoke to the college alumni and townspeople on: "The Mental Capabilities of Woman and a Plea for Her Higher Education." She said, "A young lady's mind should be garnered so well with seed for future usefulness, that even in the desert of life, she can find enjoyment and companionship in her books, her truest friends. . . . No inferiority on account of sex is observed in childhood. . . . That [woman] shall not be educated in common with man is a disgrace to the age in which we live."

> *"There have been thirty-seven Presidents of the United States, thirty-three First Ladies and innumerable Presidential sons and daughters. There have been thousands of White House staff members and a dozen or more press secretaries. Every four or eight years, the American political system moves them on, and the house fills up again. But until it has happened to you, and suddenly you are outside the fence like any tourist, you are unaware what it was really like to 'do time' in the White House."*
> —*Liz Carpenter*

This legacy was not wasted on Liz Carpenter. Such an enlightened environment positioned her for her own emerging role in the twentieth century.

When she was seven, her mother moved to Austin to be near the university so that her children could avail themselves of a college education. Liz took to the University of Texas like a cowboy takes to boots. Majoring in journalism, she became the first female vice-president of the student body in her junior year. Before that, she had graduated from Austin High and was editor of the school newspaper, the *Austin Maroon*.

After graduation in 1942, Liz headed for Washington. Marrying her college sweetheart, Leslie Carpenter, she set up housekeeping and took a job with the UPI as a reporter. Her first press conference was when Franklin Roosevelt was president. He was also the first president with whom she shook hands. But he was not to be the last.

President Roosevelt's wife, Eleanor, also impressed Liz with her stand on the social equality of women. Liz was to remember her crusade in years to come.

Liz and Les Carpenter organized their Carpenter News bureau in Washington, reporting for a string of southwestern newspapers. Balancing her role as wife to Les and mother of Chris and Scott, Liz became the first woman to serve as an executive assistant to a vice-president of the United States— a man with whom she would be associated with for the rest of his life—Lyndon B. Johnson.

Liz was riding in the motorcade the day President John F. Kennedy was assassinated in 1963. That same day Vice-President Johnson became president of the United States. And one of the first things he did was ask Liz to join him and Lady Bird Johnson in their new duties. When asked what job she wanted, she told Mrs. Johnson, "I want to be your press secretary." With that, Liz was thrust into a situation about which she knew very little. She said it was "a crash course in everything. You regretted any moment you slept and any invitation you turned down." Commenting on Liz's appointment, Lewis Gould later said, "The appointment represented a key development in the institutional history of the position of the first lady. No previous presidential wife had appointed a professional journalist to serve as her press secretary."

Being a press secretary for the president and first lady made her an instant "spokesperson" at the White House. That meant she was the bridge between the First Lady, the two daughters, Lynda and Luci, and the outside world. Most people might be intimidated by such responsibilities, but not Liz Carpenter. Rather, she said, "Show me the eye of a bureaucratic storm and I head right into it."

She said her title was clear enough as press secretary and staff director to the first lady, but when people asked her to explain what she did she answered, "I help her help him." Lewis Gould's foreword to Carpenter's *Ruffles and Flourishes* added this: "To her duties, Liz Carpenter brought a rollicking sense of humor and boundless energy. During the five years in the White House, Lady Bird Johnson enjoyed very favorable press coverage, and it was a tribute to Carpenter's good relations with the journalists who covered the first lady."

Liz describes this in many fascinating ways in her book, *Ruffles and Flourishes*. No matter where the stories started, at the White House, or the LBJ Ranch in Johnson City, Texas, Liz was the point person. She was the spark plug that produced and executed Mrs. Johnson's whistle-stop tours. She was the lightning rod that coordinated the daughters' weddings. She handled the press for state dinners and helped write speeches for both the president and Mrs. Johnson. She likes to quote, "Washington is the only asylum run by its inmates."

This was especially true when Luci Baines Johnson became the first White House bride in fifty years. Liz almost buckled under the unforeseen mountain of details. She said, "The perils of Pauline were pale compared to my cliff-hanging life with Luci and her press following."

Liz categorizes the perils into six major crises:

"TWAS THE NIGHT BEFORE CHRISTMAS."

On Christmas eve, at 11:30 P.M. exactly, Mrs. Johnson and Luci called Liz in Washington from their ranch in Texas. They told her that Luci was engaged to Patrick Nugent. Fearful someone might tip off the media before the news could be properly worded, they insisted Liz control the leaks by orchestrating the release. Only she was to do the honors. Liz quickly contacted an assistant to Bill Moyers, who was then

President Johnson's press agent. The two of them wrote the press release according to the Johnsons' wishes. By the stroke of midnight the news hit the wires. On Christmas day Luci's story was page one.

"BEWARE OF GIFTS."

Immediately, gifts began pouring in to the White House. Obviously, rules had to be made to discourage this extravagance. Liz took charge and set the parameters. The chief of protocol was to discourage foreign governments from sending gifts. Also discouraged were gifts from strangers. Those that came in were immediately returned, as well as gifts from commercial firms. Doilies and potholders made by little old ladies were accepted. Otherwise, it was to be only a family and friends affair.

"MY WAR WITH *WOMEN'S WEAR DAILY*."

The wedding dress and the bridesmaids' dresses moved to summit importance in the fashion world. *Women's Wear Daily*, as well as hundreds of other publications, wanted exclusives. They wanted the names of the layout artists and designers. Luci wanted no one to know what her dress looked like before her husband-to-be saw it. Liz became the go-between. Keeping the press at bay and the first family happy was a twenty-four-hour job.

"I WAS MARTYRED FOR ST. AGATHA."

Being Catholic and interested in nursing, Luci and Patrick wanted to place Luci's bridal bouquet at the foot of the patron saint of nursing, Saint Agatha, as they departed from the church. The search was on for a statue of the saint. Washington had a limited supply. Liz rejected the first one—too tall. She rejected the second one—too heavy. As luck would have it, there were some artisans at the National Gallery of Art shaping up two saints, one bronze and one plaster. The bronze one won, and she became Saint Agatha.

"IN UNION THERE IS STRENGTH."

Back to the Wedding Dress. Luci sought Priscilla of Boston to make the dress. The only problem was that she operated a nonunion shop. When the AFL-CIO organizers heard about it, they screamed "foul." Imagine the president of the United States allowing his daughter to be married in a gown without a union label! Liz set up damage control tactics. Nothing worked. She finally negotiated a compromise. Priscilla would design the dress, but it would be "assembled" at a union shop.

The wedding finally took place among much pomp and circumstance. Then Liz Carpenter hit her sixth crisis:

"ANOTHER WHITE HOUSE WEDDING."

Lynda was to marry Chuck Robb. Same song, second verse. Details, details, details. After their wedding, Western Union called Liz and told her that on the wedding day alone, 25,300 words were filed over their wires: UPI sent 5,500 words and thirty-eight pictures; AP sent 3,750 words and sixty pictures; *National Geographic* transmitted 350 prints to news agencies from Moscow to Tokyo. Such was the extent of media coverage for the White House event. And all of it spun out of and from Liz's office.

When Luci's and Lynda's weddings were over, and the major and minor crises had passed, President Johnson said, "Liz the whole thing couldn't have been more perfect. It was just great. You took more hell than anyone. But then, you should have, because you're in the Hell Department." Liz was gratified. She had announced to her office staff when she learned about Luci's wedding and her role in it that, "It's going to be a long hot summer with rioting in the East Wing."

President Johnson's administration was noted for the War on Poverty and his platform of the Great Society. Lady Bird made forty-seven trips across America, not only to help people see the value of Head Start and other components of the war for social justice, but also to promote her beautification program for America. This led to the famous mad and merry whistle-stop campaigns across the country, masterminded and coordinated by the funny lady with a walkie-talkie in her hand.

Trains are a happier place for Liz than planes. Liz is terrified of flying. But, let a train roll and her heart begins to beat to the *click-clack* of the wheels, and the thrill of bands playing "Happy Days Are Here Again."

Liz's duties were multiple and exhaustive for the whistle-stop train ride in 1964. Since it was in advance of the upcoming elections, the job took on chaotic proportions. Liz directed the advance men and women to arrange for the Lady Bird special whistle-stop campaign. She coordinated more than two hundred reporters who wanted to cover this type of campaigning. She worked closely with Mrs. Johnson, preparing remarks for all forty-seven stops. Only certain city and state officials were to board the train to meet her or present her flowers. Signs had to be made, as well as banners. And balloons had to be everywhere. Campaigning with the president's wife for the beautification of America and the War on Poverty was like staging a circus. But Liz was equal to the task. She admits freely that she is "a political animal by nature, a Southerner by birth, and a P. T. Barnum by instinct."

Back in the East Wing of the White House, Liz set up what she called the White House Humor Club. It met every Monday at 5:00 P.M. for the purpose of writing jokes for the president. Normally, the president had a dozen or so speech writers, but not all of them had a turn for humor. Liz picked out the five or six better known humorists and lured them into her den. The Humor Club would do their work, then send the results to the president. In subsequent speeches a little joke at the beginning always served Mr. Johnson well. Liz knew that if the president got a belly laugh from a live audience at the start, he knew he had his audience in the palm of his hand.

On March 31, 1968, no one was more shocked than Liz Carpenter when President Johnson issued his unexpected statement over television that he would not seek reelection. Liz couldn't believe he meant it. For several weeks she and other loyal supporters worked to get him to change his mind. But he never did. As she had been with the Johnsons at their entrance in the White House in November of 1963, she was there to say goodbye on January 20, 1969, when the president and the first lady boarded the plane for the last time heading back to Texas. Her great adventure with the president of the United States was over. Liz's life was about to change.

Reentry into the real world was not easy for Liz Carpenter. She worked briefly for Hill and Knowlton International as vice-president of public affairs, speaking across America. One day, while she was away from Washington on a speaking tour, her second life-changing event occurred. Her beloved husband, Les, died. Only fifty-four years of age, Les died without warning of a heart attack.

As a result Washington no longer held the magic it once did for Liz. She said, "With Les gone I didn't feel Washington was my town anymore." It was time to return to Texas. Her children were grown. Her roots and kinfolk beckoned her back. So Liz returned to Austin, bought a house, and set up shop. She would continue writing and speaking as long as she could. Little did she know that her political life was not over.

When President Jimmy Carter came into office he established the United States Department of Education. Shirley Hufstedler was named its head. Immediately after her confirmation Shirley called Liz and said, "I need you." Without hesitation Liz packed her bags and returned to Washington as the assistant secretary of education for public affairs. When asked why she took this appointment Liz said, "Because I was one woman who knew how to cut through the Washington bureaucratic red tape."

Liz's primary duty was to travel to the states which had not ratified the Equal Rights Amendment and to push for its passage. She traveled either alone or with Erma Bombeck, Elly Peterson, and occasionally Alan Alda. She became one of the primary spokespersons for women's equal rights.

Becoming a speech maker was nerve-racking at best. Writing words on paper was one thing—delivering them before an audience was something else. Liz now was the speech maker. Before a speech Liz would become tense and irritable. So she devised a plan. When she went on stage she would joke to her audience, "I was so pleased when your president invited me to speak to you tonight. He assured me that he would provide a friendly audience and a potted palm. I told him what I really needed was a friendly palm and a potted audience." The Humor Club had paid off.

Never one to be a sideline sitter, Liz put her heart and soul into speaking and rallying for ratification of the ERA around the country. For fifteen years, starting in 1971, Liz, as a founder of the National Women's Political Caucus, urged women to run for public office and campaigned for them. It wasn't easy getting sixteen innocuous words, "Equality of rights under the law shall not be denied or abridged on account of sex," through Congress and then ratified by two-thirds of the state legislatures. It passed the Congress, but did not carry enough states to become part of the Constitution. Liz regrets that the women's movement is now "on hold." But everyone knows that Liz and her friends started something that cannot be stopped.

Ready, once again, to return to Austin to live out her life with friends and family and bask in her outdoor Jacuzzi, Liz started writing *Getting Better all the Time*. In it she describes how quickly her life slowed down. Accustomed to activity and constant night life, she found herself a widow, single, and lonely. Parties were held in Austin, but mostly couples were invited. Not to be outdone, since she loved parties, she decided she would host parties herself and invite whomever she wanted—singles, doubles, and intergenerational extras. It wasn't long before she was Austin's most famous hostess. Life was still good. But soon her body began telling her it had lived too many years. When she was seventy-one, after enduring a mastectomy, developing a hearing problem, and suffering with a degenerative arthritic ankle, her beloved brother and soul mate died.

Tom Sutherland had two families. One was grown. The other had three siblings in their early teens. Upon his death, the three teenagers came to live with her.

Since 1991, Liz Carpenter, undaunted by her age or infirmities, took into her home and heart Mary, Tommy, and Liz Sutherland. Her experiences trying to understand and adjust to teenagers is chronicled in her book *Unplanned Parenthood.*

Few people have the wit or the wisdom to tackle such a responsibility. But Liz plowed into parenthood for the second round with gusto. Only this time, the rules were changed. Dealing with school activities, driving lessons, rock and roll music, and constant cooking turned Liz's life upside down from what she had planned.

She said when she left the White House "kicking and screaming, there were no regrets." She added, "I have had a whale of a time, I was never bored, and I have a restless spirit that kept drawing me to new adventures."

Her present adventure is raising three teenagers and "living to write about it." What she didn't know about teenagers, she soon discovered. "I never knew the kids of the '90s needed an appointment secretary, a medical consultant, and a full-time secretarial staff, but that's what it takes to make things efficient for them when you are into motherhood at seventy."

With the usual ups and downs of teenage traumas, Liz coped and learned and survived—so did the children. Why wouldn't she? She always said that it "never occurred to me not to work. I always wanted to be out there where things were happening. Rubbing baseboards and cooking didn't do it for me."

Now at seventy-nine years of age, Liz is still on the go. When this author called to invite her to lunch recently she was out of town for a month. The nation is still craving to hear her speeches, laugh at her writing, and enjoy her company.

When she is at home in Austin, she often sings with some sixteen men and women of the Bay at the Moon Society. And she still acts as host to hundreds of famous and not so famous friends.

One thing for sure, her "adventures" are not over. The unexpected and unplanned are constants in her life. She is eagerly waiting for the next one.

Dan Rather

D an Rather is an impish twentieth-century Tom Sawyer. He was born in a place that no longer exists. He believes that today few people even remember the Heights Annex. That's because the Annex was an isolated rural area about seven miles from downtown Houston. At the time it was touted to be the next real estate bonanza. But when Danny Rather lived there it was still so rural that few streets were paved, and most homes still lacked indoor plumbing. Today, the Annex is no more. It has been replaced by trailer homes, abandoned cars, and scrub oaks.

Actually, Dan Rather was born in Wharton, Texas, on Halloween day, October 31, 1931. His family moved to Houston when he was less than a year old. His father Irvin, "Rags," and his mother, Byrl, secured a small frame house on Prince Street in the Heights. There Danny, his brother Don, and his sister Pat grew up.

The nickname "Rags" was also passed down to Danny. Actually, he was the third family member to be dubbed with that nickname. His grandfather was the first "Rags" Rather. He came to Texas as a pipeliner for the oil fields. Irvin Rather followed in his footsteps and also "dug ditches." In those days, this was a lucrative and exciting business. The pipeline that Irvin Rather helped lay brought vital oil to the nation. The "liquid gold" helped make Texas famous and the nation mobile.

Dan Rather

—Photo courtesy of CBS News

During those early years Danny and his friends didn't think of themselves as Tom Sawyer clones. For the most part "Rags" III thought of Texas' heroes. While playing in the Buffalo Bayou, he and his friends reenacted the roles of Jim Bowie and Davy Crockett.

> *"They say that the law is a jealous mistress. I can only say that journalism is just as jealous and keeps longer hours. For those who want this life, and those who see it as some kind of glamour factory, here is what they have to know: It is a business that consumes you. You become addicted. At times I think you have to be addicted to do your job well. There is always another deadline, another story. You find yourself wanting to be there. And it eats at you."*
> — Dan Rather

Danny's first job was hawking the Sunday *Houston Chronicle* on Saturday nights. In those days boys had to stake a claim to a certain corner as there were many youngsters trying to make a dollar selling papers. This is where he learned to fend for himself and protect his "turf." He also learned that there were inequities in the entrepreneurial business. His "boss" was making money on the new subscriptions that he obtained. But, unfortunately, he failed to pass on to Danny his share of the rewards. Danny felt this was unfair. Later in life he confessed that those early years taught him some lifelong lessons: "They sharpened my determination to improve my lot and to overcome obstacles. I started shaping my own rules, and one of my first self-instructions was, 'Don't tell me I can't do this.'"

This self-made rule would be required often in Dan Rather's life. When he was merely ten years old, he began having trouble with his feet. At first his mother attributed the pain to walking barefoot. In those days in Texas it was not unusual for a ten-year-old boy to go barefoot ten months out of the year. It wasn't that his parents could not afford shoes, it was just the boy thing to do.

But the pain in his feet got worse. Soon he was having trouble walking to school. His father charged it up to growing pains and thought that Danny would probably outgrow it. This too proved not to be the case. Finally, his mother took him to a doctor.

Doctors knew very little about rheumatic fever in those years. It was a disease difficult to diagnose and even more difficult to treat. At first the doctor was unable to come up with a medical explanation as to why Danny's feet and legs hurt so badly. But for precaution's sake he told Byrl Rather that Danny must go to bed and stay off of his feet for a year. This meant no school, no football, no physical activity of any kind.

Danny spent the year immobile in bed. Reading and listening to the radio were his only entertainment. Occasionally, he would have a classmate visit. His disease lingered for five years. That is a long time for a young boy going into his teenage years. Naturally, it had its effects upon him. After five years as an invalid, Danny was thin and weak. He also was fearful of the possibility of a relapse. Every ache or pain in his knee joints and ankles caused him anxiety. There were even times he was afraid he might die.

His parents often recounted to him the story of Franklin Roosevelt, who was then president of the United States. Roosevelt had spent his adult life overcoming the effects of polio. They encouraged Danny by pointing out that if Roosevelt could overcome an affliction and become president, so could he. As fortune would have it, Danny's rheumatic fever subsided when he was fifteen, and he was finally able to go back to school.

The summer before he was to enter high school, a friend of his father's offered him a job clearing underbrush for a survey company. His mother was fearful for his health, but Dan said, "Don't tell me I can't do it."

It was a hard job. Danny often felt faint and overly tired, but he survived the summer. Later, he told someone that

Dan Rather as a boy.
— Photo courtesy CBS News

sticking with the task of wheeling a scythe through uncharted territory "was the making of him."

Danny's boyhood dream was to play football. He was short, sickly, and lacked stamina. No coach would have looked at him twice. But with Texas grit and determination, Dan "Rags" Rather gained one coach's attention, and he was allowed to try out. Dan, with his speed and wit, soon proved he could play for Reagan High. He could catch a ball. By the time he was a senior, he had progressed from playing the third string on the B team to the first string on the A team. Dan was elated and thought with his athletic skill he could pay his way through college. He entered Sam Houston State Teachers College with the expectation of winning a football scholarship.

This was not to be. Dan was not strong enough. And without a football scholarship his college career was in jeopardy. He had to find a job in order to survive in college. As he was majoring in journalism, one of his professors helped him land a job at the local radio station.

This was the beginning of Dan's love of the media.

At his new job Rather became a one-man show. He reported the news, announced the sports scores, read the commercials, and wrote the ads. "Rags" Rather became an all-around reporter, and the die was cast.

Goldberg & Goldberg said in their book *Anchors* that "soon everybody knew Dan Rather—a handsome guy, his black hair slicked back in a pompadour. He was, said school president Dr. Elliot Bowers, 'ubiquitous.' He was voted 'Sam Houston's favorite' in 1952, and Junior Class President. He was a Caballero club member, raising money for the Red Cross and the USO. He emceed the 'Press-Capades' show, and hosted the Bathing Revue, where lovely young coeds vied for the crown of 'Miss Sam Houston.' He even won the beard-growing contest one year in 'Frontier Day.'"

Upon graduation from college, Dan spent a semester teaching. Then he quickly resigned to join the Marines. Dan failed to mention to the Marines his bout with rheumatic fever as a young boy. When they discovered this oversight, they had no other choice than to boot him out with an honorable discharge.

Back in Houston, Dan landed a part-time job at the *Houston Chronicle*, as a reporter. They soon shifted him to its affiliate, KTRH radio. He became the radio weatherman.

Texas is noted for its hurricanes starting around the beginning of September. So Danny was not surprised to learn that on September 5 the U.S. Weather Bureau began tracking a low-pressure system in the Caribbean. It was the beginning of Hurricane Carla. Dan immediately contacted his boss and suggested they get to Galveston to cover the big blow when it hit. When given the go-ahead, the two men went to Galveston. They jerry-rigged a link-up of their operations to the CBS television affiliate KHOU by a primitive radarscope. This was new technology in 1961. Fortunately, it worked, and they began broadcasting just hours before the storm hit, warning residents to evacuate the area.

Dan Rather in his days as a radio reporter.
— Photo courtesy
CBS News

The great storm made landfall on Monday morning. The first blast of seventy-five-mile-per-hour winds initially knocked out the reporters' transmitter. They reverted to emergency power, while a brave engineer climbed the swaying tower and replaced a hook in the microwave dish.

For three days Rather manned the microphone. The image of Dan clinging to a tree, while describing the murderous storm, is now a part of television history. Walter Cronkite, with CBS in the New York studio, was tracking Rather's report. When he saw Dan wrapped around a tree he said, "Rather was up to his ass in water moccasins." The picture and the quotation have followed Dan throughout his journalistic career. One might say this scene made Dan famous. Or rather, it was his tenacity and display of courage that caused the executives at CBS to take note of him and call him to New York.

Dan Rather joined CBS in 1961. After a short stint in New York, he was returned to Dallas as chief of its Southwest Bureau. The civil rights movement was capturing the imagination of the media, and Dan did extensive coverage on the activities of Martin Luther King. It was also during this time that the announcement came that President John Kennedy was to make a Dallas stop on his Texas tour.

With less than three weeks to prepare, CBS made plans. In order to provide full coverage the network decided to place film drops strategically along the path that the president's motorcade was to follow. The reporters would rush the film back to the studio as soon as the president passed by. This would give them quadruple coverage from four separate sites. It was a good, quick, efficient plan.

Rather's position was on the other side of the railroad tracks beyond the triple underpass, thirty yards from the grassy knoll in front of the Book Depository building.

The motorcade was late. Rather was getting restless. Suddenly, a police car sped by him, taking a wrong turn. Then the presidential limousine passed like a blur. He did not see the president. He did not hear the shot, but he knew instinctively something was not right. He hotfooted it back to the station. Within minutes, at 12:34 P.M., a teletype copy came across the wire. It read:

KENNEDY SERIOUSLY WOUNDED PERHAPS FATALLY BY ASSASSIN'S BULLET.

Rather called Eddie Barker of KRLD. Eddie was stationed at the Trade Mart, waiting for the president. He had just talked with the chief of staff of Parkland Hospital, who reported that the president had been shot and was dead.

Another teletype:

DALLAS, NOV. 22 (UPI) — PRESIDENT KENNEDY AND GOV. JOHN CONNALLY OF TEXAS WERE CUT DOWN BY AN ASSASSIN'S BULLETS AS THEY TOURED DOWNTOWN DALLAS IN AN OPEN AUTOMOBILE TODAY.

New York reporters were waiting for Rather's confirmation. Walter Cronkite was standing by. Dan was reluctant to announce the president's death as a fact until he was sure. He called the hospital. All doctors were busy. Again Dan talked to Eddie Barker. In one ear Eddie was repeating what he had heard at Parkland. A voice came back. "What is that?" Dan thought it was Eddie. The voice said, "That's my information, too. That he's dead." The voice was not Eddie's, but a New York radio editor.

Immediately Dan heard himself say over CBS radio, "The president of the United States is dead."

Dan was sweating. Was he right? Or was he wrong? His career? His life on the block? Had he reported too soon? Was he accurate? The fear of every reporter was running rampant in his heart. He knew he was right—but what if . . .?

A little after one o'clock, Dallas time, a doctor, Malcolm Perry, covered the body of President Kennedy with a white sheet. At 1:33 P.M. Malcolm Kilduff, the assistant press secretary for the president, made the fateful announcement, confirming, thirty minutes after Dan Rather had made his statement, that the president was, indeed, dead.

It was a moment unlike any other for Dan Rather and the rest of the country.

No question but Dan Rather did exemplary reporting. During those four dark days, Dan was persistent and dedicated to reporting the news, not only as it happened, but with accuracy and fairness. It was no wonder that most of the country's television viewers were constantly glued to CBS, listening and learning from Cronkite at the desk and Rather in the field. With so much confusion, so many rumors, so many questions concerning a possible conspiracy or a potential attack on the country, the people of the United States wanted and needed answers. The fact that Rather bird-dogged every rabbit trail of innuendo and worked round the clock for the truth gave assurance to the American public night after night. It is because of such serious reporting from journalists like Dan and his fellow CBS Texan, Bob Schieffer, who was at the *Fort Worth*

Star-Telegram at the time, that a grieving society began to stabilize.

Few people realize that whereas the country had four days to deal with the shock, watch the funeral, and finally get back to work, Rather stayed with the news, working steadily night and day. It was only on the following Tuesday that he had time to reflect on this memorable occasion and mourn like every other American.

In the mid-1960s Dan had a short stint as London bureau chief, followed by becoming the Saigon bureau chief in 1965. Rather was also White House correspondent during the LBJ administration in 1964 and 1968, as well the entire tenure of President Richard Nixon.

For the next twenty-five years, Dan reported from virtually every country on the planet, from Africa to Vietnam. It is safe to say that his most famous reporting from Africa was the Somali famine and U.S. intervention in 1992. In 1990 Dan was in Iraq reporting the invasion of Kuwait by Iraq prior to the Persian Gulf War.

In 1965 and 1968 Dan's primary tours of duty for CBS were in the jungles of Vietnam. Dan was in fatigues one day and a suit the next. Walter Cronkite was the evening news anchor and received direct film reports from Rather for the six o'clock news. Often these reports were given from the "paddies," those wet fields where rice is grown.

Because of his many foreign assignments through the years, he later reported to the *Dallas Morning News* that he lives the Boy Scout motto. He is always prepared. In his suitcase are: "two suits, three dress shirts, half a dozen ties, two work shirts, a bush jacket, blue jeans, waders, a sweater, a windbreaker, thermal underwear, un-thermal underwear, a poncho, a parka, a trench coat, a tuxedo, gloves, lace-up boots, sneakers, and dress shoes."

Meanwhile, on the domestic front, the Democratic National Convention was scheduled to be held in Chicago.

The year was 1968. The Vietnam War was heating up. There was civil unrest. Mayor Richard Daley had promised President Johnson that if the convention was held in Chicago, all would go well. He vowed, "By God, I can run my town and I'll prove it."

But history recorded otherwise. Hippies, yuppies, students, and other demonstrators were clubbed, gassed, and beaten by the police on a nightly basis. Federal troops were deployed and lurked on the outskirts of the city ready to make their attack upon the demonstrators. The convention hotel was sealed off by police carrying nightsticks.

At the convention Dan Rather was on the floor interviewing delegates while Walter Cronkite was in the booth directing the CBS report. Suddenly, Rather noticed a scuffle. Four or five tough-looking characters were trying to force a delegate off the floor. Rather pushed with his microphone into their midst and asked what was happening. He was quickly pushed aside. Noticing the delegate was from Georgia, he felt he must try again. Dan squeezed in and asked, "Sir, stop for a moment and tell me why these men are treating you this way."

The next second Dan Rather took a heavy blow to the midsection, lifting him off his feet and sending him into the crowd. Cronkite had been observing the confrontation from his sky box. He ordered the cameras to focus on the scuffle, particularly on Rather. For a few seconds Dan was on the floor out of the vision of the cameras. Only heads and flailing arms were seen by the television audience. Rather struggled to gain his footing. As he tried to untangle himself from the wires and cords of television paraphernalia, Cronkite came on the air and immediately dubbed the troublemakers "a bunch of thugs down there." He anxiously queried Dan about his physical condition. Rather answered as soon as he could find his breath: "Don't worry about it, Walter, I'll answer the bell."

But all was not accolades for the hard-working journalist. One problematic incident was his encounter with President Richard Nixon. The Watergate scandal was boiling upward, and Nixon had been on the road trying to gain grassroots support in order to show Congress that he was too popular to warrant an impeachment hearing. At a press conference in Houston, Rather's hometown, Nixon was in especially good humor and had been needling Dan before the questioning began, perhaps hoping to avoid unpleasant questions about Watergate. However, when Rather stood to ask a question, the hometown audience cheered him, and Nixon jokingly asked Dan, "Are you running for something?" Dan, always quick to respond, retorted, "No sir, Mr. President, are you?"

The president actually laughed, taking the remark in a kidding spirit and seemingly not as an insult. However, some who witnessed the exchange over television took it differently and complained that Dan had been "rude." Dan admitted later that probably he should have swallowed his words. Regardless, many remember it as a slap in the president's face. But a review of the videotape shows this was certainly not the case.

This unfortunate line remains a gash in Rather's upward career, but it has not permanently scarred it. Dan had earlier gone with President Nixon to China on a now historic trip. Gradually, Dan began to understand and respect the president, covering him, as he did, closely and steadily for over five years. Then came the culmination of Watergate. And a United States president was forced to resign.

Through it all Dan Rather's aggressiveness and dedication to his craft won him other top jobs at CBS. First as a reporter for 60 Minutes and later anchoring the weekend news. When the beloved Walter Cronkite retired, Dan Rather was ready to take over his seat as chief anchor for the CBS Evening News.

Later, he hosted the weekly documentary program 48

Hours. For a time Connie Chung co-hosted the *CBS Evening News* with Dan. When their ratings began to slip, and it was clear that neither Dan nor Connie was entirely comfortable with the set-up, a change was made. As a result Connie chose to resign from CBS, taking a maternity leave until her contract expired, and Rather resumed the prime spot alone.

Dan has certainly had his ups. He has also had some downs. In 1988 he and Vice-President George Bush, who was campaigning for the presidency at the time, clashed on national television. The Iran-Contra scandal was a serious matter and Dan was probing for answers that Bush had been "stonewalling" in previous interviews. As any tough, independent reporter was obligated to do, Dan shot a direct hit. Uncharacteristically, Bush replied with fervor: "It's not fair to judge my whole career by a rehash on Iran. Would you like it if I judged your career by those seven minutes when you walked off the set in New York? Would you like that?" The vice-president was referring to an incident in Miami when Rather walked off the set of CBS just before going on the air. He was protesting a decision by the network manager to allot some of the evening news time to a tennis match. Dan had to find a telephone to call New York to ask why a tennis match was being allowed to take over the evening news time when the real news was Pope John Paul II making his first visit to the United States. Had a telephone been next to the anchor site, Dan would have avoided the delay. As it was, the network was off the air for six minutes. Ever since there has always been a telephone next to the anchor site.

At the outset of the Persian Gulf War, Dan was the first U.S. anchor in the Middle East after Kuwait was invaded. He landed the first crucial interview by any U.S. news organization with Saddam Hussein after the invasion. It was during this interview that Saddam said he believed war with the U.S. was inevitable and that the U.S. had no stomach for the heavy casualties his armies would inflict. He had learned something from Vietnam: "You can't stand the blood."

Rather continued in the Middle East, anchoring from Jordan, U.S. bases in Saudi Arabia, and other critical locations. In the meantime, he undertook a relentless diplomatic campaign, often at the risk of his own life, to liberate four CBS News personnel who had been taken captive by the Iraqis. The prisoners were correspondent Bob Simon, producer Peter Bluff, and their camera crew.

Dan was also one of the very first reporters inside Kuwait City after the coalition forces liberated it. For these exemplary services Rather won a plethora of awards and citations. And CBS credits Rather's Gulf War reporting with their rise in ratings after years of cutbacks and failures.

When the coup ousted Gorbachev from the presidency of the Soviet Union, Dan was ready to go again to cover events in Moscow, but CBS News management decided against it. Instead of placing himself in the middle of the actual scene, he allowed other foreign correspondents to make their reports complete with expert analysis. Rather, as managing editor, coordinated all their coverage, then decided on the fairest, most pertinent, and most accurate accounts which needed to reach America's living rooms.

In 1999 Dan Rather is still the anchor for CBS. He is known by some to be arrogant, cold, and unfeeling. He admits, "I don't take the bridle well," a throwback to his Texas roots. But from those closest to him he is just the opposite. One of his producers, Bill Madison, who is also a Texan, says, "Dan is generous to a fault, courtly as an old-time Southern gentleman, profoundly (sometimes embarrassingly!) sentimental, so patriotic he cries when he hears the national anthem or the Gettysburg Address; he melts when he sees a baby. He's devoted to his wife and kids, and unswervingly loyal to his friends. He will miss a fancy dinner party to visit a sick colleague. And if he knew I was telling you these things, he'd be mortified. The guy I know (eleven years) is NOT 'unfeeling.'"

But Dan believes that "you appear to be on television what you are," and he regards himself as simply a broker of information—no more, no less.

"The mark of a professional," he says, "is his ability to [be objective] over a broad spectrum of work in the same way that a professional boxer is trained not to show when he's hurt."

"I can't remember a time when I didn't want to be a reporter," he says with a Texas accent that the East Coast has spent thirty years trying to launder. Yet hard as they try, they can't wash Texas out of his blood. Even today, when he is ready for R and R, he and his family fly back to Texas. His daughter, brother, sister, and their families still live in the state. Dan and Jean keep a home in Austin.

"What Texas gave me is a feeling of independence. The people I grew up with were never impressed by anyone or anything. These were people who had to deal with the realities of life. They were not born to privilege or place: If you make it, if you survive, you're not better than anyone else— but not less than anyone else.

"I have a sense of that."

Jim Lehrer

Most Texans know Jim Lehrer from his newscast *every* evening on PBS. He has become like an old friend. Yet few know that he is first and foremost a bus freak, as described in his book, *A Bus of My Own.* If you ask him to dinner some evening he will, without much more than a slight invitation, begin to spiel out the names of the towns on the bus route from Houston to Dallas in the form one hears at any bus station. Through the years he has amassed one of the most extensive collections of bus memorabilia in America. Next to his family and reporting the news on the *NewsHour,* Lehrer loves buses.

Jim Lehrer was born on May 19, 1934, in Wichita, Kansas, the son of a bus station manager, Fred, and his wife, Lois. No doubt the baby, Jim, sucked up exhaust fumes in his first breath for he has had the infection all his life. His father, Fred, worked for a bus line, but had, in the back of his mind, the desire to own his own line some day. He believed in the American dream; all you needed was a good idea and a willingness to work.

When Jim was a young boy, Fred left his job as station manager to follow his dream. He established the Kansas Central Lines. The company started with only three buses, duly named Betsy, Susie, and Lena. They were used Flxible Clippers, some ten or twelve years old. Fred employed one

Jim Lehrer
—Photo courtesy of Don Perdue

driver plus two stand-by drivers. Their job was to make a daily trek from Wichita to Marion, a journey of about 125 miles over non-paved roads.

Jim would often tag along for the ride, sitting on the front seat next to the driver as if he was the copilot. He longed to be the driver himself.

Unfortunately, Fred's business went under in a little over a year due to the high cost of repairing the buses and a low passenger rate. Saddened by the failure, he moved his family, and all they possessed, by bus to Beaumont, Texas, where he managed the Trailways bus depot.

It was in Beaumont that Jim Lehrer began his writing career. When his teacher complimented him on an essay he had written for an English class, the idea of a career in writing emerged. He had found something that he could do which suited his physical stature and personality. Jim was never good at sports or music even though he longed to excel in those fields. Writing looked as if it could be just the right ticket.

Before long the family had to move again. Once more they packed up their belongings and boarded an old Flxible Clipper en route to San Antonio. Jim's dad had taken a job as senior solicitor for Continental Trailways.

"We believe journalists can have a professional and adversarial relationship with the people they cover that does not have to be mean or confrontational. We do not see ourselves as Mr. District Attorney, with the job to prosecute publicly within the limits of the law all persons holding public office or pubic opinions. Our job is to question public figures about their actions and views, but to do it in such a way that our audience can judge their veracity or worthiness."

—Jim Lehrer

By now Jim was in high school. When he became one of three editors of the school's newspaper, he knew he was destined to use words, one way or another, the rest of his life.

After high school Jim enrolled in Victoria Junior College and took a night job at the bus station. Between his duties as ticket agent and calling the bus' departures, he pulled out an old upright typewriter and began writing short stories.

He also wrote to several universities seeking admission, especially the journalism school at the University of Missouri. The school rejected his application, citing the lack of credibility of Victoria College. This puzzled Jim, so he appealed to his dean. The dean was furious as well as insulted. He wrote to the president of the Missouri school and challenged him. He requested exams of every subject upon which the journalism school harbored doubts. Victoria would administer the exams to Jim to prove both the viability of the institution and the worthiness of Jim Lehrer. The University of Missouri responded positively. They sent a representative to Victoria to oversee the exams. The results spoke for themselves. Jim was not only admitted as a full-fledged junior, but was exempt from any grammar or foreign language requirements. Jim felt this was one of his greatest achievements. Again, his career path was reinforced.

But his love affair with buses stayed with him. He became the local authority on bus calls, spewing out names of bus stops on the routes operating out of Victoria. Since he had them memorized, he was often asked, later in life, to perform at parties and social affairs. "This is your first call for the Continental Trailways five-fifteen P.M. Air Conditioned Silversides Thruliner to Houston from Dallas. . . ." His friends didn't need comedy acts; they had Jim to entertain them. His soliloquies would link a string of small and large communities in a breathless spiel. It was the one thing he could do that no one else at parties could. It became his stock in trade.

After forty years, he can still do it.

It was also during these years at school that Jim began to collect bus memorabilia: signs, toy models, ticket punches, baggage checks, matchbooks, uniforms, and a host of other bus-related objects. No other person in America can claim the volume of items equal to Jim Lehrer's aggregation. He calls it "The Collection." *Smithsonian* magazine published an article featuring this vast collection, including pictures of cap badges, "Safety First" stools used to help people board the bus, and many bus line insignias.

On another level, Jim Lehrer claims he inherited two important traits from his parents. The first was genetic. Both paternal and maternal families were German immigrants, his mother's father being a noted preacher in the Nazarene Church. On the paternal side, they were Catholic and Lutheran. The second important influence in Jim's life was the Marine Corps. Jim's father had been a Marine in the early twenties. So in the fifties, when the Korean War was hot, Jim volunteered for the Marines before he could be drafted into the army.

For three years Jim endured the rugged life of a Marine, thirteen months of it stationed in Okinawa. He learned several important lessons in the process. The first is "I discovered that I, a small-muscled male of barely average size—five-nine, 155 pounds—with no athletic skills or special coordination or stamina, could accomplish stunning physical feats, just because somebody ordered me to and I had no choice but to do them." And the second thing is, "the best thing about being a Marine is being a former Marine."

In July 1959, now as a civilian, Jim Lehrer took his first newspaper job. He was hired as a night rewrite man at the *Dallas Morning News* for $82.50 a week.

For ten years Lehrer worked as a typical newsman. At the start, he mostly covered stories about death. In his autobiography, *A Bus of My Own,* Lehrer describes some of these people: "They died in plane crashes, head-on auto wrecks, tornadoes, flash floods, house fires, love triangles, hold-ups, cop-and-robber shoot-outs, loaded-gun accidents, knife fights, wife and child beatings . . . I saw and smelled some of their bodies and interviewed some of the people who loved them.

"I learned about heroes.

"I learned that even murderers, con men, sex deviates, burglars, embezzlers and bank robbers have faces and family. So do their victims. So do the police officers, deputy sheriffs, FBI agents, prosecutors, defense lawyers, and judges who work the cases. So do the people who run for office, who work in district and county clerk offices, who collect taxes, who pave roads, who type letters, who teach school, who run corporations, who sue corporations, who picket, who protest, who preach, who pray."

A favorite place to find Jim was at the only airport in Dallas at the time—Love Field. He was there to interview the famous and prominent as they landed. Elvis Presley was one. Steve Lawrence another. One assignment sent him to Love Field to interview a Cardinal from St. Louis. Jim was excited. He thought it would be Stan Musial or Enos Slaughter. When the plane landed not one Cardinal player got off. Instead, a cardinal with the Catholic Church stepped out. He was in Dallas to make a speech. Jim was scarcely prepared for this type of cardinal. For once Lehrer was at a loss for words. He remembers he was termed the only foreign correspondent who never left Dallas.

Not everything was work for Jim. It was while he was at the *Dallas Morning News* that Lehrer met Kate Staples of McKinney. Kate is also a writer, but at the time was a junior high English teacher. They were married June 4, 1960, and now have three daughters: Jamie, Lucy, and Amanda.

After writing his first investigative series about the Communist Party in Texas, the John Birch Society, and the civil rights movement, he quit the *Dallas Morning News*. It seems someone in the paper's hierarchy killed his stories, and it made Jim angry. Even though Kate was pregnant with their first child and not working, Jim quit as a matter of principle.

Fortunately, the *Dallas Times Herald* needed a reporter, and Jim made the change.

At one point, while Jim was at the *Herald,* he was tempted to go into public relations. The executive editor at the time was Felix McKnight. When Jim approached him about the idea, Mr. McKnight stubbornly refused to allow him to leave the paper. "You are a newsman," McKnight said. This rankled Jim for a while, but he stayed where he was. Years later Lehrer saw the wisdom in what McKnight had said. It takes a good newsman to spot another good newsman and not let him get lost on the way.

While rubbing shoulders with other news personnel at the *Times Herald,* Lehrer met A. C. Greene.

Greene was the newspaper's book editor. When they became friends, Greene often talked to Jim about books and writing. The Greenes and the Lehrers occasionally met for dinner to discuss the latest books. One evening, Jim showed A. C. some of the short stories he had written. Greene complimented him, but advised him to forget short stories. Instead, he should go for a novel. The result was Jim Lehrer's first novel, *Viva Max.*

After several rejections, the book finally was published. As a surprise bonus the publishers sold the movie rights. Jim was delighted and celebrated royally. He was even more elated when he learned that Peter Ustinov was to play the lead in the movie. There was much fanfare and excitement when the Lehrer family drove to San Antonio for the premier.

Lehrer had been city editor of the *Times Herald* from 1961 to 1970, when he decided to join KERA-TV. Public television was opening up, and it held a new interest for Lehrer. His first assignment was as the anchor on *Newsroom.* Lehrer will tell you that the format was vintage 1950, but Dallas got its first serious media, consumer, and environmental reporting.

Reporters were sent out daily. That evening Lehrer would interview these reporters on the stories they had covered that day. Discussion among the reporters would follow.

Jim would then open the telephone lines for questions from listeners. This gave them viewers' feedback that proved to be invaluable. The show began with a thirty-minute time frame but, due to public interest, rapidly expanded to one hour. On occasion they did special, all-evening editions during elections and on matters of civic interest, such as heated debates from the city council or the local school board. This proved so successful that they began interviewing national figures who came to Dallas. Jim remembers such notables as Buckminster Fuller, Ella Fitzgerald, Harry Reasoner, and I. M. Pei, the architect.

Lehrer had discovered a news niche unique in the industry and was soon invited to Washington to work for the Public Broadcasting Service.

At this juncture, Lehrer readily admits that timing was everything. The Lehrers' move to Washington coincided with the beginning of one of the most controversial events in American history—Watergate. Lehrer privately and publicly thanks Nixon, Liddy, Hunt, Dean, Colson, Halderman, and Ehrlichman for helping him and public television gain national attention.

When Sandy Vanocur left the network, Lehrer inherited his job of news reporting. Robert MacNeil was already on board with the network as the PBS anchor. PBS opened up their channel to the senate Watergate hearings, and the American people became fascinated by them. Glued to their television sets, Americans watched Robert MacNeil and Jim Lehrer with increasing regularity.

Then came the *MacNeil-Lehrer Report*. The fact that the *Report* format only allowed a single subject matter to be taken in-depth set them in direct contrast to the brief synopsis type of reporting on the other networks. The format allowed for personal interviews and analysis on the appointed subject matter with both sides of the issue explored.

The *Report* had a different audience from the beginning. Their intention was to go for the more thoughtful listener—

discussion and dialogue were the means of gaining insight and viewpoint. *Time* magazine dubbed it "TV's best discussion of public affairs" program, regardless of the number of viewers it had attracted.

In 1983 the *Report* became the *MacNeil-Lehrer News-Hour*. Now several subjects were scheduled in the new time frame. The *Los Angeles Times Book Review* reported, "America's political leaders have come to see the *NewsHour* as a haven where they can chuck PR and confess at least some of their real stands on the issues."

MacNeil and Lehrer became fast friends and like-minded journalists. In Lehrer's memoirs, he tells us, "We both believed that Getting It Right was the first rule of journalism. Reporters and editors who use or permit imprecise language, imperfect sourcing, sweeping generalities, sarcasm, cheap shots and smug morality in straight new stories should be run out of the business. We both believed the American people were not stupid . . . and were convinced they cared about the significant matters of human events—war, poverty, corruption, government and news." They also agreed it must be fun.

The show has won many awards, including the Emmy. And Jim Lehrer has become a friendly face every week night. As Mark Harris, of the *Los Angeles Times Book Review*, says, "Lehrer on my TV screen these recent nights remains as I have always known him, rational, reasonable, straightforward and unemotional, respectful of the news-worthy people with whom he converses, and responsible to the facts insofar as they can be known." Few people in either private or public life can ask for higher acclaim.

Two major events have affected Jim Lehrer's life in more recent years. The first was a heart attack. Detailing the attack in his book, Lehrer reveals that, not only was he unprepared for illness, but he was terrified of hospitals. Both his father and mother had entered hospitals for surgery and never returned home. When he learned after several weeks of recuperation from the heart attack that he must return to the hospital again for open heart surgery, Lehrer panicked. His wife, Kate, and the girls, together with friends, rallied around him. Their comfort and positive attitude strengthened him and helped him through the ordeal. In the process, Jim Lehrer's thinking changed. There was life beyond work. And even after he was home and well into recuperating, Jim questioned the wisdom of returning to broadcasting as his love for writing novels returned.

However, the fascination of sitting before a national audience every evening on the *NewsHour* lured him back. He still observes one habit formed by his heart attack experience. He takes a nap every day.

His novels also began taking off. Although he will always be best known for co-achoring the *NewsHour,* Lehrer has written *The One-Eyed Mack* series. These books are about a Kansas teenager who lost his eye due to the sharp edge of a kicked tin can and became lieutenant governor of Oklahoma. Lehrer is now working on his twelfth novel. He recently told the Friends of Richardson Library that he has a story in him for the next thirty years.

He also writes plays. A memorable moment in his life came when he went to Jackson, Mississippi, to consult with Eudora Welty on his play *Church Key Charlie Blue.* Ms. Welty said about Jim's play, "As we watched the audiences at this play, I've sometimes wondered if they always knew they were laughing. Anyway, they were moved, there's no doubt about Jim's work that [what] moves them is his ear for dialogue."

Finally, Jim has written two memoirs. The first, *We Were Dreamers,* details his early life and experiences in the bus business. The second book, *A Bus of My Own,* revisits many of his same early experiences but moves to his adult life and his work as a nationally renowned and venerated journalist.

In 1995 Robert MacNeil decided to retire. On October 23 of that year the name of the famous program changed to *The NewsHour With Jim Lehrer.* Was there a difference after the change? Not really. Lehrer says, "We're not going to move away from hard news. The network newscasts are losing audience share. We've doubled ours in the past five years. People keep asking me if we're going to be more like them. I wonder why one of the networks doesn't decide that it has nothing to lose by being like us."

"Like us" is a real distinction. "The long stories are our front page," Lehrer says as a way of describing that distinction. The audience views the anchor as a man behaving like a gentleman in front of the cameras. He is civil to his guests. Their questions are hard, but the knife is not aimed at the jugular. Information from both sides of an issue is the objective. Dialogue is the preferred format. Fortunately, the network has given Lehrer complete authority over what is presented and how it is presented. The stories range from hot political issues to the more subtle domestic ones. They take on international issues as well as domestic interests by using interviews, debates, and panel discussions.

A writer for *Harpers* magazine once said of the *News Hour,* "It's a show dedicated to the proposition that there are two sides to every question, a valuable corrective in a period when the American people had finally decided that there were absolutely and definitely not two sides to every question . . . There is a concern for ideas rather than video images . . . and they accord us the unusual media compliment of not telling us what to think, but allowing us to draw our own conclusions after we weigh conflicting views." Consequently, more than thirty-five million people watch the *NewsHour* program each weekday evening.

As this is being written, Jim Lehrer still appears nightly on the *NewsHour*. He is continuing to write books (surely another is coming out this year), and he is still diligent about his bus collection. His latest is a "bus of his own." It is sitting in his garage.

Linda Ellerbee

ed Koppel said of Linda Ellerbee, "The woman is raucous and irreverent and writes like a dream. Furthermore, she has captured what George Burns once described as the essence of good comedy: 'Sincerity! If you can fake that, you got it made.'" Perhaps this is why Linda is hailed as TV news' smart angel.

Linda Ellerbee's life can be summed up in the phrase "The perils of Linda." Very few people have had a more colorful, up-and-down life than she. Now in her fifties, she has survived four marriages, numerous firings, alienation from her mother, alcoholism, and a bout with cancer. Still, Linda is a welcomed sight on television as an honored professional. Often outspoken, brash, and controversial, she has survived and is now feted for her role as one of the pioneers of women in television journalism.

Linda Jane Smith was born August 15, 1944, in Bryan, Texas, the only child of Ray and Hallie Smith. When she was four years old, her family moved to Houston, where she attended public schools. In those days Linda declares she was a tomboy and a loner. "I just didn't fit into any particular group, and I think I wanted to. I was the kind of kid who'd bad-mouth the idea of homecoming, and then be really hurt when no one asked me."

Linda's outlet was books. She was an avid reader. Her

Linda Ellerbee
—Photo courtesy of Gordon Munro

mother encouraged her to read to stretch her mind. Linda was also a fledgling artist. She won several awards for her paintings while in high school, including a scholarship from a local art museum to pursue a career in art.

Even at this young age, Linda seemed to be her own worst enemy. She declined the scholarship. She convinced herself she would never bean artist. Writing, she thought, was easier. One wonders what her life might have been had she pursued an art career, but we will never know. Linda enrolled in Vanderbilt University in Nashville, Tennessee, majoring in history.

"There were no journalists in my family in Texas. They all worked for a living. I did not see THE FRONT PAGE as a child; nobody I knew wanted to grow up to be Hildy Johnson, although several people I knew wanted to grow up and be Lyndon Johnson."

— Linda Ellerbee

While in the university, she tested her writing skills by submitting an essay in a contest conducted by the United Methodist Church. The prize was a summer's study in Bolivia. As a non-attending Methodist, she argued in her essay that if she were sent to the church's mission in Bolivia, then she might be converted back to organized religion along with the native Indians. This struck an evangelic response with the Methodists. She won the contest and spent a summer learning more about life and herself than she planned.

Before Linda graduated she married her college sweetheart, Mac Smith. The two of them left for Chicago, where Mac was attending graduate school. Linda started working as a disc jockey. Under the pseudonym of "Hushpuppy," she worked at an all-jazz radio station. This was her first media exposure.

Six months later she divorced Mac and set out for San Jose, California, on her own. Her new job was program director of a small radio station. This job was also short-lived. Her mother was sick. Linda felt she must return to Houston to care for her. While she was in Houston, she met her second husband, Van Veselka. A daughter, Vanessa, was born while they were in Houston. As soon as they moved to El Paso, Texas, their son, Joshua, was born. In 1971 the family moved to Juneau, Alaska.

Linda describes their Alaska experience as living in a commune in the economic sense. She said, "Some people got religion. I got politics, let my hair grow, took off my shoes, put on an old army jacket, marched, sang, lived in a commune, learned how to kill and dress deer, learned I didn't want to do that, talked revolution, walked the woods in Alaska . . ." When interviewed on her experience there, she told Tony Kornheiser of the *Washington Post,* "A couple of us had full-time jobs. The rest were writing out the plans for the new society. I knew this most surely—that certain people did the work and certain people sat on the couch saying, 'Far Out!'" Life was hard in Alaska, with few modern conveniences. Soon, Linda's second marriage was on the rocks. Politics and ideas got confused with marriage. The marriage lost.

Left abandoned in the cold country with two children, no money, and no job, Linda dug deep within herself for the means to survive. She told Jennifer Allen of *New York* magazine, "That's where all my ambition comes from, knowing I had these two little hostages to support." She immediately secured a job with a local radio station to put bread on the table. To supplement her wages she began writing speeches for Terry Miller, then the Republican majority leader of the Alaska State Senate.

But Alaska was not home to Linda. It was too cold. She longed for the sun of Texas. She said, "I wanted to look at yellow, red, and brown; I was tired of mountains, I wanted sky." Finally, in 1972, she persuaded the Associated Press bureau in Dallas to test her for a job as a news writer.

Reluctantly, the AP gave her a chance. And Linda headed back to her home state.

It was while she was at the AP that the infamous "Letter" was written. Not intended for general publication, at the time, this inflammable letter caused such an upheaval that it changed her life. The story goes like this:

Late one evening, Linda wrote a personal letter to a friend on her office computer. Within the letter were strong, disparaging remarks about Dallas, the AP, and the Vietnam War.

Linda Ellerbee in younger days.
— Photo by Bill Head
courtesy of Linda Ellerbee

She printed the letter, mailed it, and went home. The next day, members of NASA were visiting the AP. In order to demonstrate their new electronic equipment to the visiting dignitaries, an AP man haphazardly touched a certain key. Ellerbee's damaging letter appeared on the screen, then inadvertently hit the wires of newspapers in four states.

Linda was sacked. She reported, "I was fired only because the AP's legal department told them it absolutely was against the law to shoot me, no matter how good an idea it might be." She can be classified as either a victim or the victor of the new electronic age.

All was not lost. The controversial letter had its way. Although the letter infuriated some, and offended many, it also amused others. Linda found herself somewhat of a celebrity. The news industry was now aware of the name Linda Smith.

So much so that the Houston CBS television affiliate, KHOU-TV, sought her out. They offered her a job with a salary twice the size of the one at AP.

Linda had survived another one of life's setbacks, standing up. She was breaking into television.

While in Houston, she married Tom Ellerbee. In time, WCBS-TV offered her a job in New York as a reporter. Tom encouraged her to take it. This could be her big chance. Linda made the move.

After only three years she advanced to the National Broadcasting Corporation (NBC). She was now taking on network television.

Trying to prove herself as a capable woman reporter, she interviewed world leaders and ordinary people, writing and producing stories on a daily basis. She became NBC's *Nightly News* correspondent in Washington, covering the House of Representatives. The air was getting lighter at the top.

In 1978 she began anchoring and writing the script for the magazine show *Weekend*. It was on this show that Linda set her now famous signature line, "and so it goes." The tag line also became the title of her first book.

Linda's career was progressing, but her third marriage was ending. Again, it was difficult to manage work and family life. But she had set her course, no matter how bumpy or unorthodox.

Being unorthodox was Linda's stock in trade. Both in her dress and her verbal delivery she flaunted her message against the established order of things with flare and a "don't give a damn" attitude. She would show up for work in jeans, T-shirts, and sneakers. Sometimes even barefoot. And her news delivery was a blend of modish poetry and wry humor spiced with irony.

Linda is highly intelligent and insightful. Her interviews and commentaries reveal that. She is also iconoclastic, off the wall, and often irritating. She said in her book, "When things go wrong, as they often do in covering politics, Washington, crime or other pleasantries; when things are dumb, as they often are in television, local and network; when nothing works right and stupidity rules—well, it makes for fine story-telling."

But *Weekend* had rating troubles. Formatted as a Saturday night, once-a-month, issues program, it floundered for an audience. It was moved several times to other time slots. Yet it never got more than a cultist following and finally died. Linda was moved to another program, *Overnight*. This show quickly gained a loyal audience of artistic types, truck drivers, factory workers, and, believe it or not, a cadre of journalists. When the network announced that they were going to cancel the program, thousands of protesters deluged the network with letters, telegrams, and telephone calls. They even picketed NBC's corporate headquarters. But management stuck it out as they reported the program was losing $6 million a year. An ironical honor came when a few months later *Overnight* was awarded the Alfred I. DuPont-Columbia University Award, the most prestigious prize in broadcast journalism.

By 1984 Linda Ellerbee had several failed magazine shows under her belt. What was one more? NBC tried again. This time the program was called *Summer Sunday USA*. Its format was a mixture of news, feature stories, and interviews. Unfortunately, no matter how good this program was, its demise was pre-set. The network had scheduled it opposite the award-winning *60 Minutes.*

After the show folded, Ellerbee thought it was time to leave NBC. She hosted and produced a five-minute Friday episode entitled *T.G.I. F.* on the *Today Show,* and she had a brief co-anchoring spot with David Brinkley. Discouraged and unable to execute an acceptable contract with NBC, Ellerbee became a free agent.

To her surprise both CBS and ABC wanted her. After a short tug-of-war, she finally settled with ABC with a three-year contract worth $1,500,000. She would be the host and writer of the prime-time series *Our World* and would write and produce *T.G.I.F.* for *Good Morning, America.*

Our World had a new format. It used archival footage and eyewitness commentary to recreate eventful moments in world history. The show lasted only one season. In a state of frustration Ellerbee quit network television.

When asked why she quit, she simply answered, "The reason is everything." Actually, Linda was going through a hard period. She was angry at the cancellation of the show, but more than that she viewed herself as a "significantly unpleasant human to be around." She also wanted to start her own television production company. Most of all, she needed rest.

Ellerbee spent that summer in a hammock, watching the news. For once she wasn't writing the news. Summer ran into winter, and winter ran into summer. It was 1988, and the Republican and Democratic Conventions were coming up. CNN called. They needed her stylish commentary. At first she declined their offer, but when they told her she could speak her mind on whatever was important to her, she agreed.

Hollywood also called. Their interest involved producing a movie of her book, *And So it Goes.* The project failed to materialize because of an inevitable difference of opinion on what a biographical story should be. Hollywood said Linda did not understand their work. Linda said Hollywood did not understand her work. A Mexican standoff ensued.

This episode typified Ellerbee's true character. Ever the non-conformist, she nevertheless maintains a reputation as one of the best writers and most intelligent newscasters in the business. Her fans say that she is remarkable because of what she isn't. She isn't blond, pretty, thin, or stupid. Her brunette hair is generally unkempt. Her oversized glasses usually look too heavy for her face, and her casual clothes are more than casual on her size fourteen body. She likes what she looks like and makes a point of making it pointed. When asked for a comment on how she looks, she will generally mutter, "and so it goes." But David Owen, in his articles in the *New Republic*, said that, "Ellerbee is presumed on the basis of her waistline to be a brain . . . and she has no compunctions to saying, 'And so it goes' is a cliché with which she responds to the clichés that constitute her worldview. Congress is a circus, politicians are clowns, doctors and lawyers are thieves, reporters are thieves and deadbeats, life in irrational television is unreal."

Linda Ellerbee
— Photo by Rolfe Tessem
courtesy of Linda Ellerbee

Ellerbee did start her own production company with a partner, Rolfe Tessem. They named it Lucky Duck. Unfortunately, what Linda wanted to produce was not what the television bigwigs wanted to buy. The company's interest was in producing nonfiction, educational, and historical films. Linda did this on *Our World* and felt it was a successful format. Even in its short life, the program had over 32,000 teachers using it to teach history.

Balancing the company's finances on a shoestring, the partners managed to produce several award-winning programs.

On one occasion, when Linda felt that her company was about to go belly up, she did something much against her better judgment. She made a commercial, posing for Maxwell House coffee, sitting in a big easy chair next to a five-pound can of coffee. Immediately, her colleagues railed at her. They made her feel as if she had betrayed her industry. Journalists do not do commercials. Television personalities do not do commercials. Almost ridiculed out of the industry, she spent the next few months in deep depression. Looking back on the event, however, she maintains that if they knew what she knew about her own company at the time, they would have done the same thing.

Linda's depression led to further troubles. The addiction to alcohol possessed her. It became a battle she could not win alone, and she asked for help. She checked herself into the Betty Ford Center, where she spent the next twenty-eight days. When she began her last book, *Move On, Adventures in the Real World*, she had been sober for fourteen months.

Linda's life was not yet smooth. In the early 1990s she was diagnosed with breast cancer. At the time she was hosting her own television show on Nickelodeon. Tenaciously, she continued working through the agony of a double mastectomy and months of chemotherapy treatments. She survived with her humor intact. She remarked, "I lost both my breasts and all my hair. My hair grew back."

Maybe it is because she is a Texan that people call Linda Ellerbee a maverick. She likes the term and agrees it fits her. She likes being known as a bare-boned executor of words, both written and spoken. Her wry wit has punctuated her dialogue in front of cameras and behind them. Her direct, no nonsense manner has gained her a sizable following. In fact, the producers of the *Murphy Brown* television sitcom used Ellerbee as the role model for the title character. As Ellerbee says, "Murphy Brown was a wise-ass, irreverent newswoman whose smart mouth wrote more checks than her smart ass could cash. Murphy was a graduate of the Betty Ford Center, a bemused survivor of the sixties, a lover of rock 'n' roll, hater of all things disco and a helluva reporter." Once again Linda Ellerbee wrote the script.

Now in her middle years, Linda Jane Ellerbee has moved into producing children's shows for Nickelodeon. In 1992 the idea for *Nick News* was born. Linda said, "I wanted a show that encouraged kids to think and to question." *Nick News* is now in its seventh year and has won every award traditionally associated with adult programming.

For older children, ages eight to fourteen, *Nick News Special Edition* was created. This program talks with, not down to, kids about current events and serious topics of the day, such as AIDS, divorce, gun control, and television violence. Linda's guests on these shows have included President Bill Clinton, Magic Johnson, Robin Williams, and Bill Gates. In late 1998 the *Nick News Special Edition* presented "The Clinton Crisis." The program focused on the historical impact of the situation; the political and legal issues facing the president; the role the media played in the investigation; and young people's interpretation of the event. Additional issues of honesty, loyalty to family, forgiveness, perjury, and obstruction of justice were also tackled. Linda said, "When a news story becomes so pervasive that kids cannot avoid it, we try to explain it to them in a way they can understand and relate to. The potential confusion and awkwardness resulting from the public access children have been given to sensitive information about the president was the catalyst for this special. We think we can offer kids and their parents a way to discuss these issues and reduce the anxiety level that kids may have about them."

Now at the turn of the century, Linda has not given up her Reeboks or her T-shirts. Her hair is shorter, but the glasses stay. When asked recently by a *McCall's* interviewer what her advice might be to others, she answered, "A good time to laugh is anytime you can."

No telling where or when we will see Linda Jane Ellerbee next. If it was up to her you might find her "out of business and living happily on a beach somewhere. If I have to work,

I'd like to direct movies . . . good ones. Movies with a story and a nice picture."

Linda still loves Texas. She told Ellen Sweets in a feature article for the *Dallas Morning News* that, "I try to come down as often as I can. I'm still a Texan who lives in New York; that's how I define myself. When I left Houston, I literally got on the plane with one of those coolers filled with a case of queso and six dozen homemade tortillas. People think they know what Tex-Mex is in New York, but trust me, they don't."

Spoken like a true Texan.

Bill Moyers

Marshall, Texas, claims Bill Moyers as its own. Even though Billy Don Moyers was born in Hugo, Oklahoma, in 1934, Texas became his home before he could speak. Billy Don was the younger of two sons of Mr. and Mrs. Henry Moyers. His father was at one time a cotton chopper, a candy salesman, and a truck driver. In later years he became a time keeper at an ordnance works near Marshall. Although his father earned only modest wages, the family, nevertheless, lived comfortably in a two-bedroom house.

Basically, Billy Don was an all-around kid. At fourteen, this "thin, scrawny, tallow-faced boy," as his father characterized his son, went to work sacking groceries at the A & P for seventy-five cents an hour. He also played in the band, was a cheerleader, and wrote for the school paper, *The Parrot.* In his senior year he starred as the parson in *One Foot in Heaven* and maintained a scholastic average of 95.7%.

When asked about his childhood in Marshall, Moyers said, "It was a wonderful place to be poor if you had to be poor. It was a genteel poverty in which people knew who you were and kind of looked after you. Status was important in Marshall, but more important was being a part of the community."

As a child Moyers was fascinated by the radio broadcasts of Edward R. Murrow. Listening to Murrow's broadcasts from

Bill Moyers

— Photo courtesy of Don Perdue

London during World War II, Moyers says, "This stout voice coming across the ocean night after night, describing the horrors of war brought history alive to me."

After school and on weekends Moyers worked as a cub reporter for the local paper, the Marshall *News Messenger*. Upon landing the job, he immediately started using Bill instead of Billy Don because he thought the name more appropriate for a by-line.

Also while still in high school Moyers encountered a man who would help direct his life and influence in his future—Lyndon B. Johnson. Moyers told David Zurawik of *Esquire* magazine, "It was 1948, Johnson was speaking on the courthouse square in Marshall. No microphone. No loudspeaker. Took his coat off. His tie was pulled back. His white shirt was glinting in the sun. And he was literally forcing himself physically on that audience of three thousand to four thousand people there on the east side of the square. I couldn't really hear him. I was in the back row. Fourteen years old. But I remember the sheer presence of the man. And I thought, 'That's what power is. And this man is reaching this audience. And he's got this audience. And he's telling this audience something that's very important.'"

> *"Journalists are beachcombers on the shores of other people's experience or knowledge."*
> — Bill Moyers

After graduating from high school, fifth in his class, Bill headed for Denton, Texas. He enrolled in North Texas State College as a journalism student.

The first day on the campus, during English placement exams, he met his future wife, Judith Suzanne Davidson. Judith was the daughter of a Dallas railroad clerk. Since the two of them had placed at the top of the English tests, they wound up in the same literature course. As luck would have it she sat directly in front of Moyers. Bill likes to tell it this way,

"Instead of dropping a handkerchief for me to pick up, she left her books underneath the seat. The professor suggested that I return them to her, and I have been the beneficiary of that conspiracy ever since."

The two young college students were married in 1954, and now they have three grown children, William Cope, Suzanne, and John.

Bill was elected president of the freshman and sophomore classes, worked on the student newspaper, and was active in the Baptist Student Union. In his sophomore year he wrote a one-page letter to Senator Lyndon Johnson, asking him if he might work on his reelection campaign. Johnson hired him for a summer internship, telling him to learn everything he could as there were only three ways a boy could make good in Texas: be a teacher, a preacher, or a politician. Obviously, Moyers took it to heart. He made good on all three accounts.

Moyers' start-up job working for Johnson was addressing envelopes. Before long he advanced to handling the senator's personal mail. Johnson liked what he saw and took a special interest in the budding journalist. At the end of the summer Johnson was so impressed with Moyers' work that he persuaded Bill to transfer to the University of Texas at Austin in the fall.

While continuing his studies in journalism and liberal arts at the university, Bill worked as assistant news director at KTBC-TV, the television stationed owned by Lady Bird Johnson. On the weekends he preached at two small Baptist churches in the area.

In 1956 he received his degree in journalism, attaining one of the best records in the school. So good, in fact, that he won a $3,000 scholarship to the University of Edinburgh in Scotland as a Rotary International fellow. The following year he returned to the States and entered the Southwestern Baptist Theological Seminary in Fort Worth to study for the ministry. He earned a master of divinity degree there in 1959 and was accepted into the doctoral program at the University of Texas. He also received a lectureship in journalism at Baylor University.

But the ministry wasn't for Bill Moyers. He told *People* magazine, "I knew I couldn't be a preacher. I thought that my talents lay elsewhere." He told *Esquire* writer David Zarawik, "I thought it was a call to the ministry. But actually it was the wrong number." Commenting later, he remarked, "I wanted to invest my talents in the broadest possible river, and I felt that journalism and public affairs were wider and faster flowing than the ministry."

Senator Lyndon Johnson, no doubt, concurred and offered him a position as one of his special assistants in Washington, D.C. When Johnson was elected vice-president under John F. Kennedy, Moyers maneuvered to become associate director of the Peace Corps, which he joined in its formative years.

In less than two years JFK nominated him to be deputy director of the Peace Corps, one of the youngest presidential appointees ever approved.

In 1963 President Kennedy sent Moyers to Texas in November to help facilitate his upcoming visit there. While in Austin, Bill was lunching with some Texas Democrats. The date was November 22, 1963. At 12:42 a waiter summoned Moyers to the phone. On his return to the table he told his friends, "The president has been shot and is believed dead. The governor has been shot and is critically wounded. The vice-president is believed to have been wounded."

Moyers and Frank Erwin, a leading Democrat, then dashed off to a chartered plane that flew them to Dallas. On the plane the bulletin was confirmed—the president was dead. Upon arriving at Love Field, Moyers ran across the tarmac to board *Air Force One*. He had heard that Johnson was aboard. Secret Service men, not recognizing him, barred him at the ramp where Lyndon Johnson was about to take the oath of office. Moyers jotted a note, "I'm here if you need me," and sent it in. In seconds, Moyers was escorted into the private quarters of the president. He stood quietly by to witness the swearing in of the thirty-sixth president of the United States.

From that moment Bill Moyers' career spiraled. He stayed on that plane and became one of President Johnson's key assistants. Johnson used young Moyers as an organizer, expediter, speech writer, and legislative coordinator. He was instrumental in the president's reelection efforts against the senator from Arizona, Barry Goldwater. As Johnson later said, "Moyers is my vice-president in charge of everything."

It was almost unheard of for one so young to be so powerful. At the time Moyers was barely thirty-one years old. He was thin, had dark hair, and wore glasses. Most of his work was done behind closed doors, in the background, away from the public eye. Then in 1964 Bill became Johnson's chief of staff. The following year LBJ named him to the position of press secretary, a job Moyers, who preferred to work behind the scenes, was reluctant to take.

By now the Washington Press Corps was taking notice of young Bill Moyers. They were intrigued by this young divinity student, partly because of his political savvy and apparent political skills, and partly because of his character. Both *Time* and *Newsweek* featured him on the cover of their magazines —much against Moyers' wishes. He preferred to remain anonymous, believing that he could be more effective when not watched by the media on a daily basis.

The president often called him his "preacher boy." Moyers seemed to be a quick study, quiet, calm and efficient. But the president also liked to tease his youthful aide publicly about his ulcer, to which Moyers responded, "the X-ray shows it has the initials 'LBJ' stamped on it." Actually, this was all in jest as Moyers' ulcer developed while working at the Peace

Corps, but had been completely cured long before his assignment with the president.

Within time the stress on his family life, the death of his
brother, and the president's growing preoccupation with Vietnam caused Moyers to resign. Under strenuous objection from
Johnson, Moyers left his friend to become the publisher of
Newsday, one of the nation's largest suburban newspapers.

Newsday needed a face-lift. Moyers sparked new life into
the company by recruiting new and more creative writers. He
enlarged the paper with additional features in investigative
reporting and news analysis. He even changed their political
position from ultra-conservative to a more moderate stand
when the newspaper questioned the escalation of the war in
Vietnam.

During the thirty-nine months Moyers ran the paper,
Newsday was awarded thirty-three major journalism awards,
including two Pulitzer Prizes. In the meantime the owner, an
elderly man, suffered two strokes and sold the paper to new
management. The new managers promptly fired Moyers. For
the first time in his life Bill Moyers was without a job.

Days later, Willis Morris of Harpers magazine called and
asked what Moyers was going to do next. Moyers answered
that he had no immediate plans. Morris made him an offer. If
Moyers would get on a bus and travel the country for three
months, discovering the way Americans thought, he would
turn over the entire November issue for a report on Moyers'
experience.

Bill Moyers hopped onto the bus. The results were
"Listening To America: A Traveler Rediscovers His Country."
There on the cover was a large license plate on the bumper
of the bus emblazoned "MOYERS," and the entire magazine
featured Bill Moyers' experiences with the American public.
In January of the following year the report was published as
a book and became an instant best seller.

Because of this public exposure, the New York City

public television channel, WNET, approached him with the idea of reporting and hosting a weekly public affairs broadcast called *This Week with Bill Moyers*. Moyers began interviewing writers, artists, historians, philosophers, scholars, and other noted thinkers. He also produced investigative documentaries and television essays on critical issues, including his acclaimed essay on Watergate. This established him as the man who provided American television audiences with "news of the mind."

As a reporter Moyers met the great and the ordinary. His interviews with famous writers, politicians, poets, and thinkers of many disciplines were laced with reports about the lives of regular citizens. He wrote a bi-weekly column for *Newsweek* and also produced *Bill Moyers' Journal: International Report* in 1974. Naturally, this expanded the focus to leaders and writers from all over the world.

In 1976 Bill went big time. He joined CBS and served as editor and chief reporter for *CBS Reports*. Always interested in documentaries, Moyers made for CBS *The Fire Next Door*, which was an in-depth look at life in the Bronx. This won him three major awards. But not all the criticism was praiseworthy. For instance, he was the correspondent for a documentary on the negative effects baby formulae were having in third world countries where parents did not know how to use them properly. The companies who were selling the baby formulae rose up in arms. CBS News was on the hot seat and feared a lawsuit, but backed Moyers and the producers without apology. However, some of the network executives at the corporate level were unhappy with the furor. There was even more controversy when Moyers reported in *The CIA's Secret War* about efforts to assassinate Fidel Castro.

When he was filming *The Vanishing Family: Crisis in Black America*, he again butted up against the network's management. Moyers argued he needed more than sixty minutes to do justice to the people and issues in the documentary. Management told him no. Moyers threatened to quit. They settled on ninety minutes, and the American public witnessed one of the most important documentaries of the decade. Moyers considered this his most significant work up to that point.

Moyers spent two years at CBS News, returned to Public Broadcasting for three seasons, and then signed a five-year agreement with CBS, where he served as senior analyst and commentator for the *CBS Evening News* while contributing periodic documentaries for PBS in his spare time.

Bill Moyers: The Power of the Word.
— Photo: Fred Ehmann

Bill now had what he wanted—a forum to report the news plus a forum to produce serious works about ideas. He was now ready to expand beyond the political commentaries and historical essays to more erudite subjects, such as evil and mythology, which up to that time had been absent from television.

One of his most famous works is the *Creativity* series, which features a range of interviews from poets, such as Maya Angelou, to entrepreneurs, such as Fred Smith, the founder of the Federal Express Messenger Service.

Finally, in 1986 Moyers broke with CBS and returned permanently to his first love, Public Broadcasting. He told the *Chicago Tribune*, "I've always thought there's no limit to what you can do in this world if you don't want to get rich or gain

credit. . . . I've done 500 hours of television or more by staying loose, by going to where I could create an opportunity."

On his return to PBS, Moyers continued his in-depth
reporting. The first of his investigative reports was *The Secret
Government*, an exposé of the high crimes and misdemean-
ors committed during the administration of President Ronald
Reagan by the U.S. government. *God and Politics* and *The
Public Mind* explored the impact of the media on politics and
culture. His cultural interests led him to produce *A Gathering
of Men, Amazing Grace, The Songs are Free with Bernice
Johnson Reagan*, and two highly acclaimed series on poetry.

Moyers has always had a love of conversation and interesting dialogue with or without any apparent entertainment
value. To prove ideas could be popular among Americans, he
produced *A World of Ideas with Bill Moyers*. During these
thirty-minute programs Moyers met and talked with the intellectuals of our time—people whom television had neglected,
but whose wisdom could now be spread to a nation of listeners. They included authorities in fields ranging from ethics
to literature to science. It was a program designed to get
America thinking.

Moyers' curiosity about "news of the mind" led him to
Joseph Campbell, a professor at Sarah Lawrence and a
scholar of comparative literature and comparative religion.
Moyers produced six hour-long specials with Joseph Campbell discussing his ideas and research in what is the now
famous *The Power of Myth with Bill Moyers*.

Joseph Campbell proved to be one of the most inspiring
intellectuals and master storytellers ever heard on television.
Over thirty million Americans watched and listened and
learned. When the companion book, by the same title, was
released, it topped the best-seller list for seventy-five weeks.

Joseph Campbell and Bill Moyers had hit an American
nerve. During their discourse they touched on the great spir-
itual traditions of all cultures. Campbell emphasized that all

religious myths held basically the same personal story—the quest to understand one's relationship to the universe and the search for bliss, meaning the ability to live authentically in the world.

According to Moyers, Campbell would be appalled at the slick interpretation which some quarters attach to his notion "follow your bliss." Campbell simply meant that the hard, disciplined, and fulfilling task was to embrace the ancient wisdom: "To thine own self be true." If you feel the stirring to be a writer, Campbell said, "if writing gives you the deepest satisfaction, then be a writer even if you don't get rich!"

One of Campbell's former students at Sarah Lawrence said, "He was a great teacher—and an exacting one. He was a cyclone of energy before which students sat breathless in his classroom, while all of us listened spellbound." She continued, "We did stagger under the weight of his weekly reading assignments. Finally, one of our number stood up and confronted him saying, 'I am taking three other courses, you know. All of them assign reading. How do you expect me to complete all this in a week?' Campbell just laughed and said, 'I'm astonished you tried. You have the rest of your life to do the reading.'"

Moyers made conversation his format. Again, in his *Gathering of Men* and *Your Mythic Journey or Where the Soul Lives,* he sets his camera in the midst of men and women sharing their stories with each other. "It's all story," says Moyers, "whether it's verbal, whether it's visual, whether it's linear with words, it is still a way we have of trying to make sense of ourselves and the universe around us. . . . The oral tradition is the oldest, and the video medium the newest, but it's always a matter of story."

Some have said that Bill Moyers is the conscience of America, a description which causes him to bristle. *Texas Monthly* says he is "the standard bearer of the best we see in ourselves." Jennifer Lawson, programming chief of PBS, says he is a "national treasure." Jackie Onassis called him one of her heroes. Barbara Jordan went so far as to say, "I'd like to see him president."

This idea of Bill Moyers as president of the United States is not an idle comment. In 1991 there were some Democrats in Washington who had Moyers' name at the top of their list of candidates. Moyers' first response was that, "It would be fun, but for the next two years I have obligations." Actually, in 1988 there were some who advocated drafting him for vice-president. And some say it is still not out of the realm of possibility. His credentials are there. He would be a genuine outside candidate with experience in the White House, the Peace Corps, and with the public. He has worked hard to be trusted and believable.

But in 1995 Bill had heart bypass surgery, which, per- haps, canceled any possibility of the presidency. He likes what he is doing. Besides, he doesn't want to give up jour- nalism for politics.

Instead, in 1996 he gathered some of the great religious minds from every tradition together to produce a live conver- sation on the first book of the Bible, *Genesis*. A companion book followed which also became a best-seller.

In an interview with Moyers some years back, he was asked why he chose television as his means of fulfilling his journalistic aspirations. He answered, ". . . coincidence is God's way of remaining anonymous. It's as Joseph Campbell said in the series, 'When you're living your life, it doesn't ap- pear to have any pattern to it, [but] when you look back, it ap- pears as if, after all, a perfectly composed rhythm brought you from there to here.' And when I look back, I think of my life as a series of coincidences, of God's way of remaining anony- mous. And the biggest coincidence in my coming to television is that I got fired from the job that I had been doing."

Jane Hall writes in *People*, "Moyers has been honored as perhaps the most insightful broadcast journalist of our day, an astute interviewer to whom philosophers, novelists, and inarticulate workers have revealed their deepest dreams." Harry F. Waters of *Newsweek* writes that "Bill Moyers looks at America and sees freeways of the mind connecting great and complex issues, a landscape of ethical cloverleaves that affords a natural habitat for the journalist as moralist. Besides choosing fertile thematic terrain, Moyers always brings a point of view to his craft that . . . at least dares to challenge and provoke. Agree with him or not, he never leaves your mind in neutral."

To this Moyers would say, as he said to David Zurawik of *Esquire*, that he offers viewers of his productions "companionship on a pilgrimage. I think I am looked to by viewers as a sojourner, a reporter who takes them with me on assignment. . . . It's all connected: journalist, journal, journey."

During his twenty-five years in broadcasting Moyers has been the recipient of many awards and honors. The International Conference on Thinking, an annual gathering of scholars and researchers dedicated to improving critical and creative thinking, recently honored him as a broadcaster, "whose contributions to public awareness of the value and processes of thinking span multiple areas: helping the American public understand how we think, the influences that impact our thinking, and the joy and contributions that result from thinking effectively." Columbia University's president, Michael Sovern, in presenting Moyers with the prestigious Gold Baton award, the highest honor of the Alfred I. DuPont-Columbia University Award, said of Moyers, "He is a unique voice, still seeking new frontiers in television, daring to assume that viewing audiences are willing to think and learn."

His contributions to the culture of Americans is immeasurable when one considers he has produced more than 250 programming hours for our edification and written such thoughtful treatises as *Joseph Campbell and the Power of Myth, A World of Ideas* I and II, *Healing the Mind,* and *Genesis.*

In 1998 Moyers aired *Close to Home,* a five-part series on addiction and recovery. There is still more on the drawing board, perhaps a multi-part series on the South, or a four- or five-part series on Texas.

It is evident that this Texas journalist still has many miles to go before he signs –30– at the end of his page.

Sam Donaldson

S am's mother said, "Sam was always an obedient child until he went back east." Chloe Hampson Donaldson is eager to cast a favorable light upon her son. Naturally. She's his mother. But did the "East" make Sam Donaldson who he is today? Let's see.

Chloe Donaldson was left with the responsibility of raising her son solely by herself. Sam's father, from whom the son received his name, died of a heart attack eight months before Sam was born. His father was sixty-two years old.

Samuel Andrew Donaldson's father was born in 1871 in Tennessee, to a poor family. When he was only a boy, the family moved him to Texas. As he grew up he worked at odd jobs, mostly as a cowboy. Then he got a job with the railroad and worked his way up to engineer. When he had saved enough money, he bought a piece of farmland in the Mesilla valley of New Mexico, just across the border from Texas.

Sam II's mother was from Missouri and the eldest of seven children. After getting a teaching degree, she moved to New Mexico to teach school. By this time Mr. Donaldson owned a dairy and cotton farm right across the road from the school. The two met and began a courtship. When they married in 1918, he was forty-seven and she was twenty-four. Tom Donaldson, Sam's older brother, was born the following year. Fifteen years later, Samuel Andrew Donaldson II was born.

Sam Donaldson
— Photo courtesy of ABC News

"I'm a native Texan," Sam is proud to say. His mother delivered him alone at the Masonic hospital in El Paso and named him in memory of his deceased father. Three days later, mother and son went back across the Texas line to their farm in New Mexico.

What about this obedient son Sam's mother talks about? In his book, *Hold On, Mr. President,* Sam gives an altogether different story. When he was seven, he accidentally shot out the front tooth of one of the Mexican workers with his BB gun. When he was twelve, he let the horses out of their corral so he could chase them on the farm's tractor. Obedience may not have been the most characteristic term for young Sam. In his own book he describes himself as a "troublemaker."

> *"So when I cover the president, I try to remember two things: First, if you don't ask, you don't find out; and second, the questions don't do the damage. Only the answers do."*
> —Sam Donaldson

As a youngster Sam was interested in two things—radio and flying. Each evening he would sit in the kitchen and listen to the news. Often, he would pretend to be the newscaster. A neighbor friend owned and operated a ham radio. Sam was so fascinated that the neighbor taught him how to operate a ham set. When Sam was twelve, he took the examination for a ham license but failed it. Simply knowing the hands-on mechanics was not enough to pass the test.

When he was fourteen, his mother thought he needed more discipline, so off he went to the New Mexico Military Institute in Roswell, New Mexico. The first year was all but a disaster as Sam's grades were as poor as his conduct. By his second year he shifted his attitude and decided to make the most of it. He learned two things at the academy. One is that life is more fun when you are doing well, and the other is that one should never give up.

Sam fell in love with flying while at the academy. With every spare dollar he bought flying lessons. When he was ready to solo his mother refused permission. The boy was only sixteen years old. Sam was twenty-one before he could fly alone. When he did, he acquired his pilot's license.

In 1951 Sam enrolled in Texas Western, a state college in El Paso. His major was telecommunications. He will admit he was not the exceptional student he would like the public to believe, but he was still captivated by radio. In his freshman year he became a teenage disc jockey working first for a small station in El Paso, KELP. It wasn't long before he found a job at a larger local station, KEPO.

KEPO was the boot camp of radio. Sam would open up at six o'clock as the morning man and close in the evening as the final news announcer. During his last year at college, he graduated to television. He got a job at KROD-TV as an announcer. Television was more restrictive, and Sam didn't love it. He much preferred the free and easy style of radio.

When Sam was twenty, he married his teenage sweetheart, Patricia Oates, on a whim. They crossed the river one Friday night into Juarez, Mexico, and tied the knot. They had a son, Sam III, but after three years the marriage failed, perhaps due to the young couple's immaturity.

Sam Donaldson, age eighteen, working as a disc jockey at KEPO, El Paso, Texas.
— Photo courtesy of ABC News

After graduation

Sam went to the University of Southern California for graduate school. When he finished, instead of landing a job in broadcasting, he and a friend started a magazine. They called it *Television Film.* When it appeared it would take too much money to make a go of it, Donaldson sold out to his partner and returned home to wait his orders for military service. The magazine did succeed. It is still being published today.

That summer Sam had his first taste of politics. He and a friend organized the Young Republicans' club of El Paso. Since both sets of parents had been long-time Republicans, Sam espoused the Republican philosophy. He grew up believing in the protestant work ethic.

At this time Richard Nixon was the vice-presidential nominee and was coming to El Paso on a campaign stop. Sam and his friend volunteered to organize the brief stopover. They did the usual promotional exercises: renting automobiles for the parade, making signs, and illustrating banners. Sam will tell you he cannot remember what Nixon said in his speech that day, but he recalled the experience many times in the future when he met face to face with the man who finally became president.

The day after Nixon's visit, Sam reported to Fort Bliss as a second lieutenant of air defense artillery. Most of the time Sam's duty in the army was as a training officer, first in basic training, then in the deployment and operations of Nike anti-aircraft missiles. He witnessed firsthand the effects of an atomic bomb. It was a personal H-Hour.

He and another lieutenant went to Camp Desert Rock in Nevada to observe the testing of an atomic test code-named Kepler. Huddling in a trench some six thousand yards from the tower, they withstood a bomb explosion half the size of the one used to destroy Hiroshima.

A blinding light! An ear-splitting noise! A vast trembling of the earth! Desert sand and debris crashed down on them like sheets of rain, covering them from head to foot. When the all-clear sign came, they crawled to the surface of their trench to observe the aftermath. Total devastation.

The two men were immediately rushed back to camp where they were hosed down and debriefed. Sam will tell you he gained respect for atomic bombs that day. He says that they are not just another weapon. He believes that a nuclear war can never be won and must never be fought.

Three years after Sam Donaldson joined the army, he was honorably discharged. He moved to Dallas and for a brief time had a job selling mutual funds. He was neither good at the job nor liked it. And he swore he would never again attempt a job that included smiling and dialing. Discouraged, he responded to an ad for a writer for HLH Products. This was a company owned by H. L. Hunt, the Texas oilman. When Mr. Hunt interviewed Sam for the job, he asked one simple question: "How cheap will you work?"

Not knowing exactly how to respond, Sam said, "I'm not married. I have a small farm income. I want very much to work for you, so I'll work for whatever you think the job is worth to start."

He failed the test. He learned the next day from Mr. Hunt's secretary that Mr. Hunt had said that if a man doesn't know his own worth, then he isn't worth anything. Another lesson learned.

Realizing he had better get back to what he knew best, Sam applied for and secured a job at KRLD-TV, the CBS affiliate in Dallas. However, he stayed only a year in Dallas. At twenty-six years old he felt he should make his break to New York.

Unfortunately, New York was larger and scarier than he had expected. His resumé showed his lack of print experience. Sam had never worked for a newspaper. Consequently, radio or television executives were not interested in hiring him.

When out of money, he worked at odd jobs until WTOP-TV, the CBS affiliate in Washington, contacted him. Was he interested in auditioning for a summer job as relief announcer? Was he!

Donaldson was on the next train to Washington. The audition went well, and he was hired. This time his television career began in earnest. By the end of the summer he was offered a job in the news department, taking over the slot vacated by Roger Mudd, who was leaving WTOP-TV for the CBS network.

Sam was in the right place at the right time. WTOP was expanding its local fifteen minutes of news coverage to an hour, and Sam got in on the ground floor. He became a television reporter, covering the United States Senate and sometimes even the president, who at that time was John F. Kennedy. Sam would report from the field, then anchor from the studio. Writing his own material, he often did a commentary. "The Second Look" was Donaldson's first foray into news analysis on television.

Sam was enjoying his work. He also enjoyed playing.

His avocation was bridge. He had played bridge in the army, after the army, and was now playing with some sharp, seasoned players at the Dupont Bridge Club in Washington. One of his favorite partners was an older woman named Agnes Fischer. Often, they played all night. Sometimes they even played at her son-in-law's house while they baby-sat. The son-in-law's name was David Brinkley. Sam didn't know it then, but their lives would converge again, in later years, after Sam had gained as much of a reputation in television broadcasting as his hero.

During those first years in Washington, Sam met Billy Kay Butler. She worked for the U.S. Immigration and Naturalization Service. They were married in 1963. Over the years the couple had three children: Jennifer, Thomas, and Robert.

For six years Sam worked in Washington for the television station gaining valuable experience in both reporting and anchoring. In 1967 ABC called him.

At the time ABC was a fledgling network trying hard to compete with CBS and NBC. Sam had hoped for a job with one of them, but he knew it was a long shot. Although he was not unhappy in Washington working for WTOP-TV, he longed for greater glory. He never dreamed it would be with ABC.

ABC was having some internal problems at the time. The managing editors (who were running the network) were more print people than television people. They finally realized that in order to survive they must bring in new blood. Sam was, fortunately, among them. In a series of hirings they lured into their fold Frank Reynolds, Peter Jennings, Ted Koppel, Steve Bell, Tom Jarriel, and Sam Donaldson. This bold corporate move proved to be a masterstroke which ABC has never regretted.

Sam got his first scoop at ABC in 1968. Senator Robert Kennedy was flying back to Washington from New York after the New Hampshire primary. He had said he would not run for president, but Senator Eugene McCarthy had done remarkably well against President Johnson in the New Hampshire primary. Would Kennedy reconsider his position?

Sam and his photography crew met the plane. No other reporter was in sight. With ease and directness Donaldson posed the question. Yes, Kennedy admitted, he was reconsidering his decision not to run for president. Donaldson had what he wanted. He was pumped up.

Unfortunately, the network didn't jump on it immediately. They didn't break into regular programming with the scoop. By the time the evening news aired, Kennedy had discussed his decision with every other newscaster, and ABC was, once again, only a follower. Sam was disillusioned.

But experiences like this made Donaldson what he is today. He realized that ABC did not have the competitive instinct that made both CBS and NBC what they were. Nor did they have either Walter Cronkite or Huntley and Brinkley doing the evening news.

ABC was a clear third in network ratings, but to Donaldson this meant that there was more room to grow. It also meant that he, perhaps, had more opportunity for advancement. He stuck with them.

Sure enough, in 1969 Sam began anchoring the ABC weekend network news from New York. He was now working seven days a week—five in Washington and two in New York.

In 1971 Donaldson volunteered to go to Vietnam. Witnessing the situation firsthand, he said, "Vietnam was the wrong war for us. Our national interest did not require that we fight at the loss of fifty-eight thousand Americans killed doing their duty. They were sacrificed to an obsession with fighting communism wherever we found it, regardless of whether it constituted a clear and present danger to us."

When Donaldson returned to Washington, the Watergate debacle was headline news. Sam had to shift gears from the rice paddies to the halls of the capitol. Constant attention was necessary, especially during the senate hearings, and Donaldson will tell you that the Watergate story was the most intense story he ever covered. Not only was he personally fighting to gain scoops, he was fighting to be heard on television. ABC was still the baby network. Hardly anyone was listening. Their team had to work harder.

Donaldson covered the impeachment investigation. When the final vote was taken for Nixon to be impeached, Donaldson said it was a "thrilling moment." More than that, it was a "unique experience" for a political reporter. These moments come only once in a lifetime, he believed at the time.

After the emotional high of the Watergate investigation, Donaldson suffered a huge let-down. Watergate had taken much out of him. He had worked for days and weeks without rest. Now it was over. For a year and a half Donaldson was to sit back and take stock of his life and his future. Things were changing. ABC wasn't using him for special assignments as they once had. He felt left out and alone.

It wasn't until ABC assigned him to the Carter campaign that Donaldson got his second wind.

In 1976 he spent the summer in Georgia, playing baseball and visiting with the citizens. Many times his wife and children joined him.

Then Donaldson began traveling with candidate Jimmy Carter. He said his philosophy of covering a candidate was to get to "know the man, watch, learn his mannerisms, learn how to anticipate his actions, his thoughts."

After Carter's election, Donaldson continued to cover him at the White House. He watched the president move through his four years and filed some good stories. His favorite was when Carter went to Egypt and Israel, attempting to bring about a peace treaty. Everyone knew Carter was walking a thin line. It was Carter's finest hour. And Donaldson was there to relay to the American public the nuances of such a delicate and life-altering undertaking.

Covering the White House while Ronald Reagan was president established Sam Donaldson as one of television's most renowned journalists. His aggressive questions to Carter, but more especially to Reagan, placed him in the hall of fame of political reporters. Americans are now only too familiar with his line, "Hold on, Mr. President," as he took Reagan to task.

President Reagan was not noted for his ability to retain a wealth of information about a subject. He left details and facts to his staff. When asked a complicated question, he often answered with succinct yet vague answers. Donaldson never allowed him to get away with it. He wanted the guts of the question answered and often hammered the president until he got it. Now he's back at the White House, doing the same as he covers President Clinton.

Donaldson has been both praised and criticized for his impassioned—often seemingly disrespectful—confrontations with the presidents. When asked how he perceived his role at a presidential news conference, Sam responded, "My role is to ask the president a question designed to elicit his views on something of public interest, usually a program, a policy, or an undertaking of the administration, or a crisis somewhere in the world. . . . The fact that I'm addressing the president does not prevent me from aggressively asking and pursuing—to the extent allowed—questions of public purpose."

Donaldson is now known for challenging presidents. He is known for asking the tough questions, often the uncomfortable questions. Like him or not, he has become one of the best-known TV reporters in America. He was a regular panelist on *This Week with David Brinkley* from its beginning in 1981. In 1996 David Brinkley retired. Sam and Cokie Roberts now share the responsibility of hosting the Sunday morning show, renamed *This Week.*

Donaldson is aware of the controversy that surrounds him. One woman wrote to tell him, "You are rude, insensitive, crude, debasing, autocratic, unfeeling, judgmental, condescending, superior and stubborn." For Donaldson criticism is one thing—it goes with the job. But errors are another. He takes seriously the errors he makes and tries to correct them. As for the criticism, he says everyone likes to be liked, but his job is to deliver the news even if it is unpleasant or unpleasant to get. Donaldson has neither shied away from controversy nor been intimidated by authority. Remember, he once said himself, he was often a troublemaker!

In 1980 his wife, Billy Kay, told him she wanted a divorce. Sam had for many years placed his work above his family. The year he had spent in Georgia with Carter and the travels to other countries with two presidents had taken its toll. The couple separated.

For three and a half years Sam lived alone, considering himself a failure at marriage and concentrating on his work even more. His four children were his major comfort. They visited him weekly at his apartment for Friday night cookouts.

Eventually, Sam began dating Jan Smith, who worked in

Kansas City as a television reporter for the NBC station. Even though there was an age difference of twenty-two years, the two married. They both live now in the Washington suburb of McLean, Virginia. Donaldson still works hard, but not at the expense of his family.

Fortunately, Jan also loves New Mexico, where the couple frequently travel to oversee the Donaldson family agriculture business. Sam owns the farm he grew up on, along with ranch land in New Mexico. He says that is where his heart will always be, telling his fellow ranchers, "What I go back to is my hobby."

When ABC realized that the magazine format of investigative reporting (such as *60 Minutes* and *20/20*) was gaining popularity, they tapped Sam Donaldson to co-host *Prime Time Live* with Diane Sawyer. Every Wednesday evening Sam Donaldson comes into American homes hosting a program that asks the hard questions in order to uncover facts of public interest.

Former Speaker of the House Thomas O'Neill once said, "When politicians see Sam Donaldson coming at them with a microphone, they die. He's the meanest man in Washington."

It is still true; anyone who dares to come within the range of Sam Donaldson's questions must be prepared for his toxic arrows. They not only are well-directed, they are designed to rip through the established smoke screens, regardless of any potentially embarrassing impact. Full disclosure is what motivates Donaldson. If there are hidden agendas, beware, Donaldson will blow their lids off.

Today, all America easily recognizes the man in the dark suit and red tie. He seems to be the one man who can wear a cowboy hat, boots, and buckle and still not look like a Texan. It must be that New Mexico influence rubbing off. Or maybe the "East" changed him.

Bob Schieffer

Bob Schieffer is considered a faithful "deputy dog" by the CBS network moguls. A "deputy dog" is a skilled journalist minus the star quality of a superstar anchor such as Dan Rather, Peter Jennings, or Tom Brokaw.

No matter that Schieffer mans the *Evening News* when Rather is on assignment. No matter that he also anchored the *CBS Weekend News* for almost twenty years, and no matter that he still hosts the Sunday morning, awarding-winning *Face the Nation.* Schieffer is thought to be a "deputy dog."

Schieffer himself insists that the term "deputy dog" is merely an affectionate nickname given to him by Dan Rather and really has never been a term used to describe his job at CBS. "It has been a joke between Dan and me. I don't know of anyone else who has ever used the term," he said.

However, the issue goes to the question of what makes an anchorman a star. What is it that the public insists upon having in order for an individual to gain the top slot? Bob Schieffer has the looks—clean cut, wavy hair, and a compelling smile. He has the voice—a mellow tone that falls easily on the ears. He has the credentials. But Bob has never fully made it to the top. He remains a "second banana," sitting in the wings waiting for his prime-time opportunity.

The fact is that these opportunities do not often come. CBS has had only two full-time anchors in the last thirty

Bob Schieffer

years. Both Walter Cronkite and Dan Rather have held on to their seats by tenacity and stellar performance. As is the case in so many organizations, there is little room at the top.

But Bob Schieffer has made his mark. Born February 25, 1937, in Austin, Texas, he is the son of John and Gladys (Payne) Schieffer. John Schieffer was a contractor. When Bob was a young boy, the family moved to Fort Worth. He now claims Fort Worth as his home.

In 1955 Bob graduated from North Side High School in Fort Worth. Several times during his career he has returned to his alma mater to speak to the young people in that school. "Public education is everyone's business, and we must all share the cost," he once told them. "If we do not offer the opportunity for a good education to all who want it, so that each person comes to believe he has an equal chance, then eventually there will be no domestic tranquility nor any vitality in our society."

In high school Bob was a catcher on the baseball team, reported on sports for the school newspaper, edited the annual, and dreamed of being a writer or an artist. About being a teenager he says, "For the first time you're confronted with problems you'll have the rest of your life, but you don't have the experience to deal with them."

A speech and English teacher gave him the encouragement he needed. By performing in several plays he gained

> *"I don't think young people ought to adopt the attitude that all politics is dirty and it's something they don't want anything to do with. We're going to be in bad shape in this country if young people adopt that sort of attitude. What we really need is idealism and what young people have to offer. We need young people in government and the public professions, because idealism doesn't get into government by some process of osmosis."*
>
> —Bob Schieffer

confidence before an audience and soon developed a speaking style that has catapulted him all the way to a Washington newsroom.

After graduation from high school, Bob went to Texas Christian University. He majored in journalism and worked as a news reporter for KXOL until he got his degree in 1959. For the next three years he served his country as a lieutenant in the United States Air Force. He returned to Fort Worth to work for the *Fort Worth Star-Telegram*, where he was assigned to the police beat.

In 1965, still a young man of twenty-eight, Bob was sent to Vietnam to cover the war, the first reporter from a metropolitan newspaper to go there.

He landed in Vietnam armed with pen, paper, and letters from family and friends of Fort Worth soldiers. His assignment was to operate from the field, not from headquarters. Fort Worth citizens wanted to know the true situation of the war and how it was affecting individuals—mainly the men and women from their community. For four months Bob combed the rice paddies and battlefields. On his return he made several revealing observations.

"When I first went to Vietnam in December of 1965, we weren't winning the war. Then a month or so ago things started looking good. We finally had taken the offensive. We were dealing tremendous blows in the field.

"But the last week or so this has all changed. It is very possible the government of Prime Minister Nguyen Cao Ky will fall.

"If this happens, a civilian government probably will be formed and one of the first things it will do is invite Americans to go home."

About U.S. policy Schieffer reported, "Many of the men would like to hit harder. Most of the Air Force men want to bomb Haiphong. But they truly do not have the whole picture on the war and don't know what all the political upshots of bombing Haiphong would be."

In spite of these conflicting reports out of Vietnam, Schieffer praised the Americans: "I think we can be extremely proud of our fighting men. Many of them are just kids, nineteen and twenty years old. They are doing a dirty job and doing it well."

While Bob was in Vietnam, he took some rough personal shots, particularly in a riot in Saigon. The Buddhists had stirred up dissent. The elderly and the children often threw bricks and started fires. Once, they attacked Bob while he was trying to get a story, kicking and beating him on the ground. Fortunately, he was never seriously injured and returned home tanned from the sun, but thinner than when he left.

Schieffer received an Emmy Award in 1972 for a series of reports on the air war in Vietnam. This gave him the national attention he needed.

Two major events, however, had to take place before Bob was to make his way to Washington. The first was marriage.

Bob married Patricia Penrose, who had been a fellow student at Texas Christian University. Pat was the only child of Fort Worth oilman Neville Penrose and his wife Doris, both now deceased. She made her debut at The Assembly Ball in 1959. Two years later, she graduated from TCU. She is a member of Kappa Kappa Gamma. Bob is a Phi Delta Theta.

The second event was critical to many lives—the assassination of John F. Kennedy. Bob Schieffer had a particular memory of that fateful day in Dallas in 1963. He told a *Texas Monthly* reporter, "The day John F. Kennedy was shot, I rushed down to the *Fort Worth Star-Telegram,* where I was the night police reporter, to help answer the phones on the city desk. A woman caller asked, 'Is there anyone there who can take me to Dallas?' and I said, 'Well, this is not a taxi service, and besides the president has been shot,' and she said, 'Well, I think my son is the one who has been arrested.' It was Oswald's mother, Marguerite. So I gave her a ride. I always wore a snap-brim hat in those days, because I wanted to look [like] the police; if people assumed we were detectives, we'd let them believe it.

"When we got to the Dallas police station, I took her in and approached the first policeman I saw and said, 'I've brought Mrs. Oswald over from Fort Worth—is there anyplace we can put her?' They cleaned out a little office in the burglary squad room. As the evening wore on, they took us into a holding room where we were going to be allowed to talk to Oswald. Finally, Captain Will Fritz, who was the chief of homicide, turned to me and said, 'Who are you with?' And I said, 'Well, now, who are you with?' And he said, 'Are you a newspaper reporter?' And I said, 'Yes, aren't you?' That's when I was summarily excused.

"I always look on it as the biggest story I almost got."

In 1965 Schieffer received the Chairman's Award in criminal law for a study he conducted concerning the responsibility of Texas lawyers to represent indigent persons in criminal cases.

In 1966 Schieffer became local anchor for WBAP-TV, at that time the NBC affiliate in Fort Worth and Dallas. In less than two years, the job led to his coming to Washington and joining the staff of CBS News.

For some thirty years Bob Schieffer has been a familiar and comfortable face on our television sets. His warm, assuring personality, along with his compelling smile, has endeared Americans to him.

As well as being personable, he is highly respected among his peers and colleagues. The fact that he works hard, produces quality material, and maintains his objectivity has served him well in Washington. Unlike other notable anchors or television journalists, Bob is the only one who has covered all four major Washington beats: the Pentagon, the White House, the State Department, and Capitol Hill.

Fortunately, the 1960s and 1970s produced more press opportunities than perhaps any other decades in the century. The assassinations of a United States president, a United States senator, and a civil rights leader, along with Watergate and Vietnam, proved to be more grist for the mill than most journalists could ever hope for. They did not have to hunt for news. News came to them.

As anchor of the Saturday *CBS Evening News*, Schieffer reports firsthand the crises that continue to disturb America. As a White House correspondent he has become acquainted with every president from Nixon to Bill Clinton.

Commenting in 1974 about the fall of Nixon and the transition days, he said, "I think the reason the economy is in the shape that it's in is there was so little direction at the top during those last months. It's apparent now that President Nixon spent most of his time on Watergate matters."

At another time Schieffer commented, "Richard Nixon did not leave the White House because he got a bad press. He left because he had offended the American people's sense of decency and fair play, and as a result they made him leave. . . . The press did the country a great favor by exposing Watergate, but those of us in the press must never forget that if there had not been enough honest men in government willing to prosecute Richard Nixon, then the abuses would not have stopped."

Gerald Ford, the vice-president, assumed the office of president when Nixon resigned. And it was his task to nominate another vice-president. History will record that Nelson Rockefeller's nomination was shaky, but finally confirmed. Later, when Ford was planning his strategy to run for election on his own, a tactical error in timing was made. Rockefeller withdrew his name before Ford could prepare the public for it. CIA Director William Colby was fired as well as Secretary of Defense James Schlesinger. In spite of this, Ford, after a noble effort, won the Republican nomination.

However, his party did not win the election. Democrat Jimmy Carter did. Consequently, Gerald Ford is the only president who was never elected by the American people.

Schieffer was particularly fond of Gerald Ford. As a member of the White House Press Corps, Bob traveled with Ford to both Europe and China. They also traveled together to forty-nine of the fifty states during the election year. In the meantime Bob continued to anchor the Sunday *CBS Evening News* in New York. Schieffer chalked up an incredible 250,000 miles of travel with the president in one year.

During the Christmas holidays that year, Schieffer, his wife Pat, their two daughters Susan and Sharon, and other members of the White House Press Corps, joined the Gerald Ford family in Vail, Colorado, for a Christmas celebration.

Bob Schieffer frequently returns to Fort Worth. He has been awarded the Distinguished Alumni Award from his alma mater, Texas Christian University. He has also been named "Honoree of the Year" and holds an honorary doctorate from the university.

Bob Schieffer began anchoring the weekend *CBS Evening News* in 1976. This meant that he would take a shuttle to New York, leaving every Saturday morning at 10:00 A.M., and returning twelve hours later. In bad weather he was forced to take the train, making it back to Washington after 1:00 A.M.

During his tenure many historic stories hit the airways, among them the bombing at the Atlanta Olympics, the assassination of Israeli Prime Minister Yitzhak Rabin, and the crash of the Valuejet plane in Florida. It was Bob Schieffer who brought them to us.

Then on Saturday night, August 24, 1996, Bob voluntarily bade the CBS *Evening News* audience farewell. As he said goodbye he spoke of his "fine wife." Then he stated that she had told him "with a straight face" that she "really didn't mind staying home on Saturdays waiting for me to come home."

He was asked why he quit. "Simply because I know it's time. . . . I have outlasted a lot of air shuttles. When I started, Eastern Airlines—now long gone—used the old Electra prop jets for shuttle duty . . . the fare was $38 round-trip then."

Most of Schieffer's work now centers on Washington. He continues to host *Face the Nation* on Sunday mornings. Dan Rather often cuts to him on weeknights as he continues to cover Congress. And when Dan is away, Bob is a regular substitute anchor. We will also continue to see him with earphones at future national political conventions. It would not be natural without him. He has been a part of the last fifteen conventions.

Andrew Heyward, president of CBS News, says, "Bob Schieffer is one of the most astute, thoughtful and respected reporters in the business. He also happens to be a terrific anchor and a wonderful colleague. Whatever Bob wants to do around here, CBS News is better for it."

In his spare time Bob and Pat like to attend Texas Ranger games. Bob's brother, Tom, is president of the team. When Ed Bark of the *Dallas Morning News* asked Bob who has the better job, Bob answered, "He does. No question about it, especially when they're winning."

Bob Schieffer has had his share of winnings in his own game. He has received many awards as a Texas journalist in the national and international scene. Among them is the Overseas Press Club Award for best interpretation of foreign affairs, six Emmys, and, most recently, a 1995 Sigma Delta Chi Award from the Society of Professional Journalists for his commentaries on *Face the Nation*.

Bob co-authored *The Acting President*, a book about Ronald Reagan and his presidency.

In the late 1990s, Bob Schieffer, as well as Dan Rather and Sam Donaldson, were consumed by the Clinton scandal as it descended into a full-fledged trial before the Senate of the United States of America, with the chief justice of the United States Supreme Court presiding. On a daily, almost hourly, basis Bob reported and analyzed the White House reports, and evaluated the Congressional hearings and impeachment proceedings. No one realizes more than Bob Schieffer that he was mired in the midst of one of the most historic events in the history of the United States, but then no one is more experienced or capable of communicating, to the waiting American public, the true facts than Bob Schieffer. He is a Texan with a conscience. And if that is the sign of being a "deputy dog," then it is the most endearing and satisfying title Dan Rather could have given him.

Molly Ivins

C an Molly Ivins really say that? It's a question many ask. Not only can she. She does. Molly Ivins is the first female journalist to cover Texas politics with the cattle guard down. Texas is her beat, and the "Lege," as she calls the Texas Legislature, is her fodder.

Molly Ivins, a consummate journalist with a beef about everything that is unjust and phony, is a Texan through and through, even though she was born in Monterey, California, in 1944. When she was four, her parents moved to Texas from the Chicago area. And when Molly was a teenager, they moved to the posh River Oaks section of Houston, Texas.

Her father, James E. Ivins, was the general counsel for Tenneco Oil Company. He was a proud man, ambitious, and a conservative Republican who served in the military during World War II. Molly's mother, Margo, was from a privileged family, but left all affectations with the older generation. Molly talks about her mother in her book *You Got to Dance with Them What Brung You,* and says, she "was a gay and gracious lady, and also one of the kindest people I've ever known. In eighty-four years of living, she never mastered the more practical aspects of life—I believe the correct term is 'seriously ditzy,' but she was nobody's fool. A friend of mine claims that my mother must have been the model for the Helen Hokinson cartoons in *The New Yorker,* that was her

113

Molly Ivins

— Photo courtesy of Tomas Pantin

type, but she was as shrewd as she was ditzy. It was like living with a combination of Sigmund Freud and Gracie Fields." Molly's mother died early in 1998.

Molly grew up with a silver bit in her mouth, then spat it out after she learned that established, southern, conservative folk wisdom was not necessarily wisdom. She attended public school in the lower grades, then went to St. Johns, a private high school in Houston, and then Smith College in Massachusetts. The adage "the apple doesn't fall far from the tree" didn't apply to a girl like Molly. Instead, she ventured as far away from her roots as the law would allow. In fact, she jerked the roots out of the ground. Today she is a quick-thinking, beer-drinking liberal who often thumbs her nose at anything and everything dubbed "establishment." Hers is a broken branch from her conservative, southern family tree. Conscious of this, she dedicated her second book, "To my mother and my father, for whom it has never been easy to be related to me, love and gratitude."

> *"There are two kinds of humor. One kind makes us chuckle about our foibles and our shared humanity. The other kind holds people up to public contempt and ridicule—that's what I do. Satire is traditionally the weapon of the powerless against the powerful. I aim only at the powerful. When satire is aimed at the powerless it is not only cruel—it is vulgar."*
>
> — Molly Ivins

Being an exceptionally bright child, she noticed that when the adults in her life told her not to drink out of the "colored" water fountain because it was "dirty"—she knew that something was amiss. Already, her experience contradicted what her own society told her. In truth, the "white" water fountain had stains and chewing gum splotched over it while the "colored" fountain was clean. She thought, "What's going on here? They are telling me something that isn't so." Large questions remained in her mind. In fact, Molly Ivins, the maverick journalist, has based her entire career on questioning the traditional way of viewing the world. Although she will tackle any issue, politicians are her specialty—especially the ones in the Texas Legislature.

It was obvious early on that Molly was not going to be a conforming southern girl. It is true that at one time, as a teenager, she thought her future would consist of getting married, having five kids, and being a famous foreign correspondent. But as a voracious reader her world enlarged. Issues such as race, feminism, civil rights, and politics fascinated her. She began to see the irony, as well as the inconsistency and inequity, in what she read over what she was told and saw. Perceiving what so few others understood, Molly began to develop counterpoints in satirical metaphors. Instead of allowing anger or bitterness to color her thinking, she captured, then capitalized on the foibles and follies of everyday human experience. Molly rebelled against the redneck, East Texas, Bubba conservatism.

Being almost six feet tall as a sixth grader helped to mold this attitude. She says she was the "Too Tall Jones of her time—a St. Bernard among greyhounds." In other words, "It's hard to be tall and cute." Consequently, she was more comfortable playing basketball than cheerleading. Nor did she fit the Junior League profile of a young girl desirous to "come out" as a debutante. She has never married because the men she liked never asked her.

Her first taste of journalism came while working two summers in the complaint department of the *Houston Chronicle* while still in high school. Here she learned about readers' interests, what they demanded from newspaper writers, and what piqued their disapproval.

After graduating from Smith College with a degree in history and studying philosophy, language, and political science, she won a scholarship to the Columbia School of Journalism, where she earned her master's degree. The following year she went abroad to study at the Institute of Political Science in Paris.

Prepared now for her first full-time job, Molly returned to the States and snagged a job as a police reporter at the *Minneapolis Tribune*. The time was the turbulent sixties. The hard side of life was an exciting and an often dangerous assignment for her. America was in a frenzy over many issues, and Molly gained valuable insights into movements toward social change. According to Judy Jones of *WE* magazine, Molly said she covered "militant blacks, angry Indians, radical students, uppity women and a motley assortment of other misfits and troublemakers." It was a great time to cut one's journalistic molars.

But Molly was homesick. When she noticed an advertisement for a job with the *Texas Observer*, she made a decision. As she related in her book, "I [had] always wanted to go somewhere Up North or Back East or somewhere where people talked about books and ideas, or something besides the weather and football all the time. . . . And all I learned is that folks everywhere mostly talk about weather and football. So I came home."

The *Texas Observer* is a small, liberal magazine that covers the Texas Legislature as well as social issues. Molly Ivins became its editor. She had one mission. Close in on the capital. Every state official was fair game. Every issue, every bill, every debate was grist for her pundit's pen. Ivins' Texas "Lege" was about to become famous.

"Opening day, 61st session, 1971, I walked onto the floor of the Texas house, saw one ol' boy dig another in the ribs with his elbow, wink, and announce, 'Hey, boy! Yew should see whut Ah found mahself last night! An' she don't talk, neither!' It was reporter-heaven," she wrote in the introduction of her first book.

Molly had returned to the promised land.

The "Lege" was the ideal place for Molly to activate her acid pen, her rapier wit, her irreverent language, and her liberal voice. According to Mimi Swartz in an article in *Texas Monthly,* Molly "had been teaching herself how to be an *Observer* writer—opinionated, funny, unabashedly life-wing— since her adolescence; now she turned her talent on a state that was as backward, poor, and ignorant as any Third World country."

Ivins calls the Texas Legislature "the finest free entertainment in Texas. Better than the zoo. Better than the circus." In her columns she lampoons politicians, bad mouths their decisions, and publicly exposes their underhanded games. She once commented that if a Texas congressman's "IQ slips any lower, we'll have to water him twice a day."

During the six years that Ivins worked at the *Observer*, she occasionally gave the "Lege" a break, opening up her column to a wider range of political topics. They included "national politics, government scandals, the sanctity of football in Texas, country music, a group called Debutantes for Christ, feminism, and the idiosyncrasies that make Texans different from other Southerners and Southerners different from other Americans."

For reasons Molly can no longer remember, and now wonders why, in 1976 she turned in her press badge to the floor of the Texas Legislature. The *New York Times* called to offer her a job. She buckled at the honor. Plus the money was better.

At first Molly thought working for the *Times* would suit her temperament and journalistic style, but even so, Molly didn't like it. "*The New York Times* was a great newspaper; it is also No Fun," she reported in her book.

After a year of covering various political beats in the Big Apple, Molly was ready to move on. She was invited to join the national staff of the *Times* and prevailed upon her employers to relocate her anywhere but New York. They chose Denver. Molly became the Rocky Mountain bureau chief in 1977, covering nine states. Rarely agreeing with the more formal style of the New York paper, her unusual choice of words and one-liners finally got her in trouble. She wrote a feature article about a community chicken-killing festival in a small town. She set the scene. People were sitting around drinking beer, listening to country music, and plucking chickens. The one-liners in the story were too much for the managers of the *New York Times*. Molly Ivins sensed their frustration and quit.

Fortunately, the *Dallas Times Herald* offered Molly a job free of restraints. She could write about topics that she wanted to, say whatever she wanted to, and use words she chose without fear of editing from the higher-ups. This was dancing music to her ears. Molly stayed in Dallas for three years. Then she moved back to Austin, bought a house, and reported in at the *Times Herald* bureau.

The *Times Herald* remained true to its word. They published the barbs and biting words of Molly Ivins three times a week. Molly Ivins became a household name. Some Texans would publicly mention that name—others could not. She was either loved or hated. The liberals loved her; the conservatives called the paper in angry protest.

Letters to the editor flooded the *Times Herald* office. Most of them were critical of Molly's sharp tongue and outrageous declarations. She skewered politicians unmercifully, and loyal readers of the paper often demanded that Molly Ivins be fired. But the *Times Herald* held fast. In fact, editor Lee Cullum told *People* magazine that, "She's our most valuable asset."

The Republicans were always an easy target for Molly. When Ronald Reagan and George Bush were in the White House, Molly's pen was mightier than the veto. She loved giving Bush a hard time about his claim of being a Texan. From her point of view, Bush resided only in Washington,

D.C., or Kennebunkport, Maine. She issued her classic line, "real Texans . . . never use summer as a verb."

While at the *Times Herald,* Molly began spreading her charm to a wider audience. In one particular month her by-line appeared in the *TV Guide, Reader's Digest, Playboy,* and *The Progressive.* She then published her first book, *Molly Ivins Can't Say That, Can She?*

Much to her surprise, Molly became instantly famous. Her book not only made it to the *New York Times* best seller list but stayed there for over six months. Expected to sell only about 20,000 copies, the book sold over 100,000 in hardcover and another 100,000 in paperback. It was Ann Richards, the second woman to become governor of Texas, who said, "Molly Ivins has birthed a book and it is more fun than riding a mechanical bull and almost as dangerous."

In her introduction to the book, Molly sums up her attitude toward Texas and its politics: "I suppose I could claim I did my best with what I had. Lord knows, Texas politics is a rich vein. Politics here is like everything in Texas, just like it is everywhere else—only more so.

"Twenty-five years of reporting on the place and I still can't account for that lunatic quality of exaggeration, of being slightly larger than life, in a pie-eyed way, that afflicts the entire state. I just know it's there, and I'd be lying if I tried to pretend it isn't.

"Being used to it has its advantages. Expecting things to make no sense gave me a leg up during the Reagan years. As for George Bush of Kennebunkport, Maine—personally I think he's further evidence that the Great Scriptwriter in the Sky has an overdeveloped sense of irony."

In her second book, *Nothin' But Good Times Ahead,* she says, "that Bush may know how to get the machinery of government to work, but since he clearly has no ideas about what he wants it to do, the point is moot." Her favorite nickname for him is "Wienie One."

Molly has fun caricaturing the main characters in the Texas Legislature. She calls former Speaker of the House Gib Lewis "the Gibber." She calls former Governor Preston Smith "POP" for Poor ol' Preston, and in an article for *Time* magazine said "POP Smith . . . was intellectually challenged by the task of getting from the mansion to the capitol every day."

She refers to former Governor Bill Clements as Dollar Bill Clements or Bill the Lip and is ruthless with President Ronald Reagan. She said, "I've been collecting euphemisms used on television to suggest that our only president is so dumb that if you put his brains in a bee, it would fly backwards." She sums up Reagan later with, "The buck stopped before it got here." Senator Kay Bailey Hutchison she simply calls the "Breck Girl."

Molly also spends her ink on subjects she basically likes, such as country music, women and football, and rich people. One of her favorite targets is H. Ross Perot, who she says is richer than God and "a man with a mind half-an-inch wide." She "once announced to an astonished world that Perot is a communist, worse, an agent of the Kremlin, on account of he had attacked the entire foundation of the Texan way of life—football. Right in front of God and everybody, Ross Perot said the trouble with Texas schools is too much football. Imagine!"

In 1990 Molly Ivins cut back from three columns a week to two to write *The Big Book,* a study of Texas politics. She thought this was the time. Unfortunately, she was unable to finish it. Noted for her iconoclastic apparel for work (and everywhere else), she returned to the *Times Herald* after the year in a sweatshirt. The sweatshirt warned, "Don't Ask About the Book." So *The Big Book* is still in the dresser drawer.

"I write Texas," she emphasizes, and in so doing sticks to a rigid, unspoken rule of honesty. She would not deliberately write something that was untrue. On the other hand, she never stops with the obvious, but embellishes it with her love of words and her dislike for right-wingers, Republicans, and phonies of whatever color or creed.

When the *Dallas Times Herald* folded in 1993, Molly was again without a job. This time there was little lag time between positions. The *Fort Worth Star-Telegram* knew a good thing when they saw it. They immediately hired Molly to continue her hilarious, irreverent, pointed columns.

In 1992 Molly finally agreed to have her columns syndicated. Today, over 200 newspapers across the country carry her work. Richard Newcombe, president of Creators Syndicate, which distributes the thrice-weekly columns, says Molly is "witty, insightful, interesting, and she offers insights and perspective offered nowhere else."

Today she often captures the eyes and ears of the nation. She hobnobs with Governor Ann Richards. She has been seen on *MacNeil-Lehrer NewsHour,* and heard on National Public Radio's *All Things Considered.* She has been on *Nightline* and recently was a guest commentator for *60 Minutes.* She is a constant contributor to magazines such as the *Progressive, The Nation,* and *Mother Jones.* She also has written for *McCalls, Time, Savvy, Ms.,* and *Playboy* as well as the *Washington Journalism Review*, and has been nominated three times for the Pulitzer Prize.

In all of her work, Molly uses her special gift—humor—to enliven and season her writing. "We're all entitled to laugh. There's far too much unthinking respect given to authority. It's much easier to be funny when you're speaking, because you can with an expression—the lift of an eyebrow or a gesture—indicate that you're just kidding. And of course, an enormous amount of humor is timing; you have to write in the pauses, which takes some skill."

In 1994 *The Nation* came out with a suggestion that "Texas liberals, who sometimes seem pathologically eager to support losers, should recruit the one person in their midst who could win the U.S. Senate seat up for grabs next year:

Molly Ivins." Most of this was tongue in cheek, and Molly took it so, but she responded in her own inimitable way.

Dear Nation Readers,

Well, it was a swell campaign while it lasted. My brief foray into electoral politics at the behest of this very magazine swept through Texas like a dose of Ex-Lax. . . . Offers to help poured in. Ed Rollins called to say he had some leftover walking-around money from the New Jersey governor's race. My pal, H. Ross, offered to lend me some old charts so I could do well in debate. And a Highly Placed Source said he knew of two former Arkansas state troopers who would be just terrific at protecting my privacy, as soon as they fulfilled their new book contract.

Well, Molly knows how to take it and give it back.

Because of her three books, a plethora of columns, and numerous magazine articles Molly has gained celebrity status. Out of the blue she was contacted by the producers of the television series *Designing Women*. They wanted to establish a character for the program modeled after her. Molly's comment was, "It strikes me as somewhere between ludicrous and disconcerting that a character in a television series would be based on me . . . I thought, 'Jesus, you're not dead?'"

Can she say that? Of course, she can.

What else from the likes of Molly Ivins?

Journalists for the New Century

In the late 1990s some Lone Star journalists began to appear on national television who will bridge the centuries. Scott Pelley, a Lubbock man, is now with CBS as their White House correspondent and reporter for *48 Hours,* and one wonders if he is not the man they are grooming to take Dan Rather's place when Rather decides to retire. There is Catherine Crier, from Dallas, who is an attorney journalist, and there is Stone Phillips, hailing from Houston, who now hosts *Dateline* on NBC several times a week. Lisa McRee, another Texan, co-hosted *Good Morning America* for a time.

These and other rising stars are faces that will become more familiar with each day on our television sets. Each has made admirable showings for which Texas can be proud. With more networks and cable companies added to our viewing choices, there will undoubtedly be new Texans coming to the television screen, editing our newspapers, and reporting on radio. We live in a world of communication, and the best communicators will be chosen.

Texans now circle the globe with their talents in the media. Writing about them will be an ongoing process.

Bibliography

Authors in the News. "Dan Rather's Career Crisis." Detroit, MI: Gale Research, 1976.

Bark, Ed. "Bill Moyers." *Dallas Morning News* High Profile, January 12, 1997.

Bernstein, Richard. "Walter Cronkite Finds It Hard to Say No." *The New York Times* Biographical Service, July 1993.

Braden, Maria. *She Said What?* Louisville, KY: University Press of Kentucky, 1993.

Brown, Les. *Les Brown's Encyclopedia of Television.* Detroit, MI: Visible Ink Press, 1992.

Burka, Paul. "The News About Jim Lehrer." *Texas Monthly,* October 1995.

Carpenter, Liz. "Salado Days." *Texas Monthly,* August 1988.

———. *Getting Better All the Time.* College Station, TX: Texas A&M University Press, 1987.

———. *Ruffles and Flourishes.* New York: Doubleday, 1970.

———. *Unplanned Parenthood.* New York: Random House, 1994.

Cockburn, Alexander. "The Tedium Twins." *Harpers,* August 1982.

Considine, Bob. "Walter Cronkite: A Personal Perspective," "Walter Cronkite, Transitions." Authors in the News, Detroit, MI: Gale Research, 1976.

Contemporary Authors. Volumes 31, 43, 111, 115, 138, 145.

Cox, Betty Wilke. *Liz Carpenter: A Girl from Salado.* Austin, TX: Eakin Press, 1993.

Crawford, Ann Fears, and Crystal Sasse Ragsdale. *Women in Texas.* Austin, TX: Eakin Press, 1982.

Cronkite, Walter. *A Reporter's Life.* New York: Alfred A. Knopf, 1996.

Current Biography Yearbook, 1986.

Dallas Morning News. Tuesday, August 27, 1996.

Donaldson, Sam. *Hold On, Mr. President.* New York: Random House, 1987.

Draper, Robert. "Dan Rather is a Good Ol' Boy." *Texas Monthly,* November 1991.

Ellerbee, Linda. *And So It Goes: Adventures in Television.* New York: G. P. Putnam's Sons, 1986.

————. *Move On, Adventures in the Real World.* New York: G. P. Putnam's Sons, 1991.

Ferguson, Andrew. "The Power of Myth." *The New Republic,* August 19 & 26, 1991.

Goldberg, Robert, and Gerald Goldberg. *Anchors: Brokaw, Jennings, Rather and the Evening News.* NJ: Birch Lane Press, Carol Publishing Group, 1990.

Jones, Judy. "The Unsinkable Molly Ivins." *WE-Women's Enterprise,* August 1996.

Lawson, Carol. "Liz Carpenter: Back on the Trail Again." *The New York Times* Biographical Service.

Lehrer, James. "The Confessions of a Wayward Bus Conoisseur." *Smithsonian.*

————. *A Bus of My Own.* New York: G. P. Putnam's Sons, 1992.

————. *We Were Dreamers.* New York: Atheneum, 1975, 1986.

Lingberg, Tod. "The World According to Moyers." *National Review,* March 10, 1989.

McClendon, Sarah. *Mr. President, Mr. President!: My Fifty Years of Covering the White House.* Santa Monica, CA: General Publishing Group, 1996.

————. *My Eight Presidents.* New York: Wyden Books, 1978.

The Nation. January 2/10, 1994; February 7, 1994.

Newsweek. September 29, 1986.

Newsmaker. Detroit, MI: Gale Research, 1991, 1993.

Nemy, Enid. "With Three, She Gets Nine Inch Nails." *The New York Times* Biographical Service, November 1994.

Owen, David. "Twinkies." *New Republic,* March 30, 1987.

Palmer, Robert. "A Southern Novelist Serves as a Muse to Drama." *New York Times* Biographical Service, February 1988.

Polier, Rex. "Bill Moyers Knew He Must Opt for Public Television." *Authors in the News,* Vol. 2.

Political Profiles. "The Johnson Year." New York: Facts on File, 1976.

Rampson, Nancy. "Molly Ivins." Newsmakers, Detroit, MI: Gale Research, 1993.

Rather, Dan. *I Remember.* Boston: Little Brown and Company, 1991.

————. *The Camera Never Blinks.* New York: William Morrow and Company, 1977.

"The Superego Colliders." *Newsweek,* September 30, 1991.

Swartz, Mimi. "The Price of Being Molly." *Texas Monthly,* November 1992.

Sweets, Ellen. "She's Not Kidding." *Dallas Morning News,* September 4, 1998.

Time. October 29, 1965.

"Taking CBS News to Task." *Newsweek,* September 15, 1986.

Wrolstad, Mark. "Donaldson and Safire Trade Verbal Jabs in good-natured SMU debate." February 14, 1996.

Index